The Book of Poo

Fun Toilet Learning for People with Special Needs

AMANDA SMIGIELSKI

Copyright © 2024 Amanda Smigielski.

All rights reserved. No part of this book may be used or reproduced by any means, graphic, electronic, or mechanical, including photocopying, recording, taping or by any information storage retrieval system without the written permission of the author except in the case of brief quotations embodied in critical articles and reviews.

Balboa Press books may be ordered through booksellers or by contacting:

Balboa Press
A Division of Hay House
1663 Liberty Drive
Bloomington, IN 47403
www.balboapress.co.uk
UK TFN: 0800 0148647 (Toll Free inside the UK)
UK Local: 02036 956325 (+44 20 3695 6325 from outside the UK)

Because of the dynamic nature of the Internet, any web addresses or links contained in this book may have changed since publication and may no longer be valid. The views expressed in this work are solely those of the author and do not necessarily reflect the views of the publisher, and the publisher hereby disclaims any responsibility for them.

ISBN: 978-1-9822-8814-3 (sc)
ISBN: 978-1-9822-8815-0 (hc)
ISBN: 978-1-9822-8813-6 (e)

Library of Congress Control Number: 2024901493

Print information available on the last page.

Balboa Press rev. date: 09/13/2024

ACKNOWLEDGEMENTS

It has taken a village, a town and two cities to raise our child so far. There are so many people we know and have to acknowledge for their help in raising our children. We have had the huge privilege of access to and enjoyment of a range of helpful individuals and institutions. These people and their wonderful interventions brought a lot of support, knowledge and kindness to our lives. More than once the medics saved a life. Thank you to you all. Thanks and appreciations go to the JR Hospital in Oxford. Special thanks to the dedicated and highly talented staff of the Children's Hospital and Paediatric Intensive Care Unit. Dr. Pike and Dr. Gada. The Oxford Eye Hospital worked wonders for our son despite his efforts to hinder progress. Thank you too to the staff of Klinikum Frankfurt Hoechst and therapists in Occupational Therapy, Speech and Language and Physiotherapy. Thank you to the educators in Max Baginsky Kindergarten, Bad Soden, Larkrise Primary School and Iffley Academy. Maite Gonzalez and Elle Poole.were outstanding and fun support for our son. .We loved attending the Children's centres locally. Here we found support, stimulation for our children, parenting education, encouragement and local parent friends. The research and work of Reuven Feuerstein offered a valuable way forward for us. The teaching, training and support given by staff at the Feuerstein Institute in Jerusalem was invaluable. Thank you to the wonderful local community in Jerusalem who took us into their hearts. Thank you to the people in the parish of St. Mary the Virgin in Iffley. Special thanks go to Patricia Lamond Michael, a wonderful inspiration and support. Thank you for your friendship. Thank you Jan Spurlock; your love, prayers, support and friendship are deeply appreciated. The charities, Down's Syndrome Oxford and Breakthrough Learning were a godsend. DSO has given our family an important community. Thankyou Vanessa Nicholls for your work to help many children with learning difficulties and introducing me to the work of Reuven Feuerstein. Dr. Kamal is a legend, thank you for all your help and guidance. Thank you to my family, near and far. The dedication, imagination and love of Dr. Philip Mann, my husband and father of our children is remarkable. Thankyou to our amazing children. The wonderful understanding and encouragement of Dr. Edward Smigielski, Helen and Chris Bannister, Kathleen Barrett, a superstar in every sense of the word for me. Thank you loving cousin Debbie Lekhouritis and friend, Alison Worlledge, who suggested I write this book many years ago. Alan Mann, Margaret Mann, Dr. Judith Mann, Alex and Ella Mann, you have shown so much beautiful acceptance, love and support. We are blessed with some wonderful fiends who have become our family. Rebecca Wrigley, George and Martha Monbiot, Louise Graham, Jane Stokoe, Zen Zdonyly and Melanie Brotherhead. You have been my strength and stay so often and are fun friends for all our family. Thank you to doctor and writer, Jane Wilson -Howarth who first looked at this work with a clear and very helpful editor's eye. Heartfelt thanks to Cecelia who edited this book and Sam Worlledge for your wonderful cover illustrations. You are all amazing and I am humbled by and grateful for your many talents.

CONTENTS

Acknowledgements iii
Preface vii
Glossary ix

PART ONE- OUR FAMILY'S STORY

1. Catching Up 1
2. A Creative Response and Practical Measures 6

PART TWO- PRACTICAL MANUAL OF INFORMATION

3. Getting Started 11
4. Diet, Gut, and Psychology 16
5. The Slower Road: Development Expectations and Patterns 20
6. Watching, Noticing, Listening: Communication and Cognitive Development 25
7. Improving Cognitive Ability 41
8. Improving Communication 51
9. Toileting and Poo-Specific Mediation: Timings and Action I Need to Establish for PIT 58

PART THREE- SURVIVAL KIT

To the Parent or Carer 63
Pit Stop Checklist Ideas 71

Afterword 86

PREFACE

I have written this short book as homage to the endless possibilities of life, love, and adaptation for parents of children with complex needs, or indeed anyone who's having trouble with toilet learning. The focus of this book is toilet learning or "training", but it will include other areas of development for you as well as your child as life unfolds for you. The aim is to support you in raising your child with some ideas and materials which were often hard won in our family's experience. My fantastic husband and I have the good fortune to have two children. The eldest, a delightful boy with complex needs and an amazing younger sister who is Neuro-typical. Both children are wonderful characters, full of curiosity and good humour. As a family we aim to enjoy life, whatever challenges arise.

This book has two main parts: a memoir and a manual, which of course intersect. The book also contains a survival kit of questions and suggestions to support your toilet learning progress. I was motivated to write this book in response to my need for helpful, accessible information about how to support toilet learning for a person with special needs. Nothing existed which addresses the wide range of considerations and information which this topic demands. As a parent and a professional teacher for over two decades, I needed to know and understand the physiological, developmental and emotional factors behind difficulties and how to overcome them. I am an experienced teacher of children with Special Needs and a parent of a child with complex needs. I have also worked as a researcher for universities in the area of enhancing cognitive development for youngsters, including those with learning difficulties. This book is a collection of information gained through academic study, professional and personal lived experience, research and relationships with wonderful learners. I've used fictional names for our children and other people in this book to protect their privacy.

You've brought your child or person this far in the world already and have learned your own necessary skills to communicate well. The person you care for may be a young adult who still needs personal care but is slowly gaining more independence here. You may already have encountered and met some unusual challenges. You've helped your child to learn about the world and achieve new skills, and now you're ready to take on toilet learning for "number two". As another person coming from a similar place, I salute you. You are now on a superhero journey! You and your child are undertaking an adventure which will require you both to reach for and grow new parts of yourselves, parts you didn't know existed.

I hope this book can be a guiding light and comfort of a kind which was not there for me as I struggled to understand and assist with my child's challenges. My aim is to share some of our own experiences and to give simple, encouraging, and practical information to support your journey with your child. I am reaching out to you with friendship and support. You are not alone. There are many of us who are gifted with these unique children. No book can give you all the answers, as the very nature of your child's condition and personality will make your experience different to that of any other. In this whole book, there may be one or two suggestions which CHIME with you and the situation you are in with your child. That is the PATH TO TAKE. This is new territory you are treading. You are making this path happen with your child as your partner.

This book will though suggest structures, tips, and materials to support you and your youngster as you figure out what works best for you in the endeavour of toilet learning. Two themes will reoccur throughout this book: the idea that *you are a superhero*, succeeding in the face of many challenges; and the need to create possibilities of meaningful motivation and learning for your child.

GLOSSARY

Before we progress, let's take a look at some terminology you may encounter as you meet professionals and do research connected with your child. This list is by no means exhaustive, and I'm sure there are many more terms I have and haven't encountered. I've also added some terms which come from the fields of psychology and education for children with SEND, such as Social Stories, intrinsic motivation, modelling, and role playing.

The terms *neuro-typical*, *neuro-diverse* and *neuro-different* crop up a lot in the literature and in speaking to professionals about your child. What follows is not a definitive description of all experiences but points to some salient features of these conditions. The more you understand about your child, the better placed you are to support them.

Autism and **autistic spectrum disorder (ASD)** are lifelong developmental disabilities that can cause significant social, communication, behavioural, and self-regulation challenges.

Complex needs people have a diagnosis of one or more conditions such as Down syndrome and autism, which has profound and sometimes challenging effects on their understanding, interpretation, and interaction with the world around them. These complex needs may affect their physical, mental, emotional, social, and financial wellbeing, interacting with and exacerbating one another and causing individuals to experience several problems simultaneously.

Contingent touch generally means the use of touch to physically guide or touch children in appropriate ways to meet a particular end, including assistance with transition, providing comfort, or preventing poor behaviour.

Intrinsic motivation "occurs when we act without any obvious external rewards. We simply enjoy an activity or see it as an opportunity to explore, learn and actualise our potentials."[1] It is the dream of all teachers to have students with intrinsic motivation—people who want to learn because it's fun and they seek to know more.

---

[1] "What is Intrinsic Motivation? How Internal Rewards Drive Behaviour," Kendra Cherry Medically reviewed by Amy Morin LCSW

Mediation comes from the Medieval Latin word *mediare*, "to be in the middle". Mediation is the practice of assisting the individual learner to build on what they know in order to change and improve the way they think. It also includes the passing on of information. Parents and carers mediate the world to children all the time through explanations and interventions in their life experience. The difference for children with complex needs, however, is that the information given has to be delivered in ways that are digestible for youngsters with SEND. These young people may not have the cognitive hardware to understand or even feel comfortable with messages given. Mediation is necessary to achieve understanding and effective communication in micro digestible steps with much repetition as creatively as possible.

Modelling is the process of learning by copying another's behaviour. It is also called **observational learning**. Humans model one another naturally. Modelling learning involves a particular kind of neuron, known as a mirror neuron.[2]

Neuro-diverse or **neuro-different** describes people whose development is not following a typical or expected path in health and development. There is notable variation in the function of these people's brains and often difficulties regarding sociability, learning, attention, mood, and mental function. The term *neuro-diversity* was coined in 1998 by sociologist Judy Singer and journalist Harvey Bloom, according to Wikipedia.

Neuro-typical is an adjective which describes a person whose development follows a typical or expected path in health and development.

Now and Next Cards are words printed on **PECS** cards used frequently in teaching to support learning activities for very young pupils and those with SEND. This gives the learner clarity and emotional security with the skill of sequencing activities illustrated on the PECS cards.

PECS, for **Picture Exchange Communication System**, allows people with few or no communication abilities otherwise to communicate using pictures. It was developed in the United States in 1985 by Andy Bondy, PhD, and Lori Frost, MS, CCC-SLP. PECS pictures support learning and communication and allow for abstract concepts such as time and sequence to be developed. **NOW and NEXT cards**, for example, work well in learning by using PECS pictures. The words NOW and NEXT on laminated cards are used frequently in teaching to support learning activities for very young pupils and those with SEND. This gives

---

[2] https://www.structural learning.com

the learner clarity and emotional security with the skill of sequencing activities illustrated on the PECS cards.

PIT (Poo in the Toilet) Campaign is the name I gave to the long and dedicated effort needed to enable toilet learning for a person who finds toileting skills very tricky to master.

Poonami is the light-hearted term I use to describe the results of our child's bowel behaviour over the years. The term emerged for me as a result of comforting banter with supportive friends. It is not original to me but does describe tricky events which were difficult to deal with several times during the day and night. A poonami is a large and unstoppable flow of excrement which would occur unexpectedly. A great deal of cleaning up and cheering up attention was then needed. At first our child was unaware of his poonamis. As time went on and he began to know what was happening, it was important not to transmit our own negative feelings. Over time we were able to move our child to the bathroom without him panicking about the transition to clean him up. The sudden and overwhelming extremity of the situation was reminiscent of the tsunami caused by earthquakes under the sea in 2011—seemingly uncontainable and very difficult to deal with. The constant need for cleaning and washing was exhausting. A bit of wordplay was a way to detach from emotions which were difficult and sometimes overwhelming. It was necessary to develop a sense of detachment from any judgement. Learning to respond in a conscious, kindly way rather than react in a panicked fashion was tough but very necessary. I am blessed with a .good sense of humour and this was invaluable in coping with very stressful situations.

Role playing is the acting out of a particular person or character, for example, as a technique in learning, training, or psychotherapy. Role playing is a play activity with endless possibilities for learning.

SEND or **SEN** is an acronym for Special Educational Needs (and Disabilities), used throughout literature and communication to describe people with learning and other disabilities.

Social Stories are short descriptions of a particular situation, event, or activity which include specific information about what to expect in that situation and why. Comic-style pictures and words are used to illustrate key information. Social Story is a trademark originated by Carol Gray in 1991. Social Stories can be used to develop understanding about a situation and therefore improve reaction and behaviour. The many applications of Social Stories include helping people to cope with changes to routine and unexpected or distressing events. There are many examples and templates available on the internet.

Spiky profile is a term usually used in schools for students who have strengths in, even compulsions towards, some areas while exhibiting difficulties or refusal in others. This is a common characteristic in the learning behaviour of children with complex needs and autism.

Transition is a change in state of being from one situation or place to another, such as movement from sitting to standing or changing rooms or activities. Transition can present very serious problems for some people with SEND. Our own child struggled with getting upstairs/downstairs, out of the front door for school, and other transitions. It was often mystifying how a simple task could present such huge problems. In schools, I worked with many youngsters with SEND who struggled to change subject, topic, place, or even page as part of a lesson plan. Transition often needs a lot of practice, reassurance, and a clear plan given to the child in advance. Visual supports such as **PECs** and **Social Stories** are helpful.

PART ONE
Our Family's Story

Catching Up

Children with complex needs have a lot more catching up to do from the get-go. My own child, Sammy needed extra help and bespoke support with everything. Very poor health in infancy impeded development on every level. All physical, intellectual, and communication development was slow—it was happening but at a glacial pace. Issues to do with breathing, epilepsy, holes in the heart, and allergic reaction to medication led to many months in hospital.

When Sammy was well enough to be at home with us and started to develop, it became clear how tricky progress was going to be. He began walking just before his fourth birthday, after years of physiotherapy. As parents, we trained in muscle development massage to promote muscle-nerve communication and function. Diligent encouragement and modelling were also part of the mix. We were helped and supported throughout the early years by amazing and dedicated NHS staff and volunteers in our local NHS Trust. Our deep gratitude goes out to these people.

We lived for a few years in Germany, where our health insurance bought a lot of physio and speech therapy with specialists in clinics and at home, following specialist training of parents. Our child also had a range of physical supports, such as a Kaye walker to improve posture, muscle tone, and confidence. There were also many hours of, calm, patient encouragement and therapy provided by medical specialists and us as parents for Sammy. I was trained in specifics about the theory and practice of relevant therapies so

I could do this work on a daily basis. I have a host of certificates from courses attended and skills honed through day-to-day application to improve our child's bodily functions and understanding of the world.

Dad also undertook as much training as possible and was a stalwart participant, leader and supporter of all fun and improvement efforts. Our son Sammy's speech is still developing at age 13. His understanding is evident and improving. Sammy still needs however, huge dollops of encouragement and modelling about how things are done. Development continues, but outside the time and space of our mainstream expectations.

I have sought and undertaken a great deal of training to learn about and meet our child's needs. I have been a highly proactive parent seeking advice wherever it could be found, some applicable and some not. Many talented professionals have contributed their time, expertise, and ideas to improving our child's abilities, and we are grateful for this. We have implemented many of the ideas we've learnt into our daily lives as far as practicable.

The premise of this book is to offer support and help with toilet learning, particularly "doing poos" in the toilet on a regular, reliable basis. We have arrived at this Holy Grail in the last two years but still encounter occasional difficulties. Our next challenge is learning to wipe the bottom with toilet roll, which is still a work in progress! We currently veer between a job well done and a job not done … and a blocked toilet with a full roll of tissue.

Learning to Be Realistic

It is not possible, however keen you may be, to be proactive on every front all the time, especially if you have other children and an employment contract to fulfil. As often exhausted parents of children with Special Educational Needs and Disabilities (SEND), we have to balance our energies and pick our battles. You may well feel overwhelmed by all the advice you're given and medical appointments to attend. My SEND parent peers all felt this way—and felt a lot of relief when we admitted it to one another. We were often struggling with difficult situations in a world which didn't understand.

Modern technology has enabled us to set up support groups at low cost and create our own communities of self-help. I am in a local WhatsApp group and am a member of Down Syndrome Oxford, both for parents with SEND children. We give one another support and share useful suggestions among fellow parents facing similar issues with our offspring. We also share fun and child development activities, insights and ideas, and emotional encouragement. It's both useful and invaluable to be open and honest and to laugh together. It's so important to know you're not alone—especially when it comes to the ups and downs of toilet learning.

In the second part of this book, we'll be looking at the classic model of toilet learning. But first I'll be honest with you: trying to follow the classic advice for our son with complex needs was a disaster! As he made his way through infancy with poor health and slow development, the dream of normal toilet learning receded from us. The slow development was not only physical; it became increasingly clear that his understanding of himself and the world was impaired. How much of this impairment was due to severe illness, and how much to his conditions, we will never know. But we had to work out another way to equip our child with basic human toileting skills. Our child did not develop any of the signs of readiness at any time.

There were so many challenges connected with his development, and sometimes it felt overwhelming. We tried to address one or two at any one time. Walking, using hands, and communication were our top objectives in the first five years. Our child had breathing and eating problems, which were resolved when he was, age 5 by means of surgery in the local German hospital, another source of amazing support. We worked on food-based skills after that. Luckily for us, our child loves food and is willing to try most things. But the toilet issue remained a problem.

Our daughter, Grace, who is two and a half years younger than Sammy was so determined as a toddling baby to use the larger toilet that she fell into it through the toddler seat. My toilet teaching for Sammy worked well for her. Our son did not take in any ideas about toileting and continued to self-soil. We began to buy bigger pull-ups, a bigger potty and continued on. .It was very expensive, not to mention not ecological. We resolved to keep trying even though we felt hopeless at times

Because we could not rely on the classic toilet learning techniques, we had to develop a whole range of strategies, including use of medication. Movicol or Laxido, forms of macrocol, was prescribed to regulate the bowel function. We stopped using the medication when our child was 8 years old and beginning to do a regular poo in the loo.

AMANDA SMIGIELSKI

Building a Mental Concept of Poo

Alongside physical difficulties came the challenges of creating the concept of "having a poo in the toilet" in our child's mind. He didn't seem to have any perception of poo, what it is, and why it's best done on the toilet.

It was a tall order. He had never really experienced poo as a separate thing from wee. We tried to show him what wee and poo looked like in the toilet. We showed him pictures found on the internet. These efforts were all equally futile. Our child was genuinely dumfounded by the strange actions of his parents and sister. We could see he wanted to please us with a response, but he simply had no concept of what we were trying to say. It seemed he would never grasp the essential idea. He was very comfortable to remain in specialised child incontinence nappies, which were onerous to deal with, expensive, and beginning to be noticed by peers as he proceeded to older years in primary school.

We did have it on our side that he urinated in the toilet, since urination was more visible to him as a boy. He could see the action even if he couldn't feel it. For a long time, we didn't know if he could feel the sensation of needing to go for a wee. It had taken six years to develop a regular practice of urination.

The autistic component of our child's experience led to many years of sleep patterns more typical of a new-born child, and nocturnal wanderings. At 3 a.m. one morning, I decided to pop my 4-year-old on the toilet, where he did a wee. He also weed in the toilet at 4.44 a.m. most nights and began to get himself on the toilet independently. This habit during the night became increasingly regular, though daytime toileting remained—inexplicably to me—much more difficult to establish.

Then at age 7, our son started to copy the boys in his class at a mainstream school. When they said they were going for a wee, it normalised the word and feeling in his mind. With wees in the toilet and support and help at both home and school for a few months, by the age of 8 Sammy was regularly using the toilet normally. He could sign his intention using Makaton (see Chapter 8, "Improving Communication") but said the word *poo*, not *wee* when a wee was what he needed.

Despite his success with wees, number two in the loo eluded us. It was clear that the methods which had worked eventually for wees were not hitting home for poos. We were still using pull-up nappies out in the world and chancing underpants only at home. A **poonami,** as we came to call it from "poo tsunami", occurred several times a day, despite or maybe because of a good, healthy, fibre-filled, probiotic-friendly diet. The need for cleaning and changing continued. Much of my waking and sleeping life was punctuated by uncontrollable outbursts of diarrhoea, like explosions, by Sammy. The constant cleaning, changing, and washing and the swift exits from social events made life difficult.

The regular event of poonamis really controlled our social possibilities. Even with the use of ever larger pull-ups, we couldn't do much that was truly spontaneous and were careful to avoid situations that might lead to judgement. In the public arena, the sympathy given to a parent with a child of 10 with bowel issues is quite different to the broad understanding you encounter if you have a toddler with a leaky bottom. It's not that people in general are unkind. It's just that the workings of our bowels and any issues around them are almost taboo—a secret world in our society. We somehow develop a set of shared understandings and expectations which we don't discuss openly. There is a strange, shared sense of disgust about this perfectly natural function of our bodies. We have a common norm for what is age-appropriate, and a commensurate sense of shock and embarrassed aversion when an individual violates that norm. A playground encounter with a distressed older child who can't communicate clearly and their panicking parent produces a situation of social dissonance.

As I quickly frogmarched my child off to the nearest(badly designed for this purpose) public toilet with a warning to other parents not to use that swing or slide, which I'd first quickly cleaned down with baby wipes, I had a ready repertoire of words to reach for. I hurled a promise into the air behind me that I'd be back to finish the clean-up job—A promise fulfilled as soon as possible. On some occasions, people offered help, and this was invaluable. Their kindness invoked tears in me as I explained with gratitude what was going on and what needed to be done. There are kind, understanding and helpful people everywhere, and I wish, readers, that such beings are the people you encounter.

Once on a trip to the north of England to visit family, a particularly bad outburst exhausted that day's supply of seven nappies and two packets of baby wipes. The challenge of efficiently changing a large child in public facilities loomed large .As a woman, I had to take him into the ladies' public toilets and bear the piteous and judgemental stares of others in this incongruous situation. I had a well-rehearsed patter about complex needs, several conditions, and a desperate need for toileting and wash facilities. I felt disloyal towards my child in explaining his existence and situation constantly to total strangers. Many people just stared, but there were others who offered help or kind words, or who directly and positively engaged with our son. These were my light-bringers, people with kind hearts whose gentleness and humour transformed difficulty for us. I thank all of you who reached out—you made a brilliant difference.

2

A Creative Response and Practical Measures

Our circumstances made us creative. We got out and about a lot and were not confined by our limitations. We wanted our children's early lives to be full of fun and adventure. We had to adapt to the challenge of poonamis in strange places and by and large were equal to the task, with careful planning and preparation. Every outing was made with a large supply of spare clothes, baby wipes, grab toys, spare nappies, and soil bags.

Despite regulating Sammy's bowel function by means of medication, a carefully timed routine, and healthy fresh food, I sometimes felt unequal to this challenge. Unrelenting nights of interrupted sleep and poonamis were taking their toll. Another trip to the north to visit loved ones went down in memory for the mega poonami that again exhausted my expanded supplies of nappies and wipes. My friends and I ended up in a lake with a stream running in and out to wash my child. I had to fashion a padded piece of underwear from the spare clothing I'd brought for the day. We laughed with gallows humour about how we would remember this absurd situation one day. Sammy will probably remember being swished around in the water and having his bum gently cleaned whilst waving at paddle-boating tourists.

With Grace, the potty training books I tried in Sammy's early childhood worked a treat. Three days from start to finish, with clear understanding and communication on Grace's part. They weren't at all applicable to our child with SEND. He just did not understand what we were talking about. At low, exhausted ebb, I prayed for help.

A New Dawn and New Ideas

Just when things were at their worst with disturbed sleep, regular poonamis, and all the attendant social difficulties, two massively helpful and influential people came into our lives. Both have a huge affection for our child .Both possess huge hearts and deep understanding and skill about child development for people with SEND. Both had a will to assist our child and us with a process which began to ease our misery and make our ambition of clean toileting seem like more than a pipe dream.

These two people—Sophia, Sammy's remarkable teaching assistant, (TA) at school, and Seren, a remarkable doctor and top mum who worked in our home once a week—used their knowledge to work on understanding how our child thought and how he could be best supported in their settings. Between us parents and this new support of such excellent quality, we began a programme of monitoring Sammy's eating, drinking, and toileting. We also implemented a fresh programme of mental/emotional support for our child. Most of these ideas and approaches are in the second part of this book, the practical manual. Regularity and repetition of procedures, along with a lot of good humour, began to yield positive results. But there were many twists and turns, and our trajectory was spiky, to say the least. A brand new curve ball was added to the mix. I had a diagnosis of MS following a sudden and catastrophic episode of poor health. Sammy was 8 years old. I had to adjust life to new patterns for my body and work out how to get better. I did find the help and information I needed to recover and manage the illness.

Feuerstein Instrumental Enrichment

Around the time that Sophia and Seren arrived in our lives, I was offered the opportunity to do a type of training called Feuerstein Instrumental Enrichment. FIE is an approach to brain training for anyone who wants to improve their thinking skills. It is particularly helpful for children with SEND. I did the training and started to implement it at home. The system is predicated on a particular psychological approach developed by Reuven Feuerstein. It uses puzzles, games, and thinking challenges to encourage the growth of new synapses in the brain.

Our reluctant-to-learn child, after the difficulty of getting through his school day, did not want to think more at home. I asked his school whether I could come in to do this work with him once a week, which became twice a week. A special room was made available to us for our FIE mediation work, which soon began to pay off as Sammy's cognitive skills improved. A marked advance in communication at home and school showed this. Sammy's medical appointments and being a Feuerstein research subject also confirmed a significant improvement in comprehension.

I worked with his dad, fantastic sister, and helpers to adapt the FIE approach to real-life situations and challenges. Sophia adapted his lesson work to include the FIE approach with very positive results. Our son still uses physical and linguistic expressions he learned at this point to communicate. It greatly improved his confidence and language skills.

The change of routine, expert support, and extra brain development work began to turn the story round for us. It was the combination of approaches, all delivered with huge positivity and interaction, that promoted a shift in our child's understanding, and I'll be sharing these techniques in Chapter 7.

Picking Our Battles and Staying Power

The physical and psychological capacities of our child posed obstacles which are not experienced in so-called "normal" development. The Down syndrome component of his development meant that Sammy's arms were not long enough to reach his bottom for many years. His privacy awareness began when he was 12 years old. This is wonderful for us as parents who wondered for so long whether this day would ever come. Now his arms are long enough to wipe his bottom, we're working on bottom-wiping as part of self-care. Our child wants to do this with his own agency—he announces, "Self!" and sends us away as his sense of privacy and what's socially appropriate grows.

The large number of issues we needed to tackle throughout the years led us to choose to work on the developments which seemed both most important and likely to succeed at the time. We worked to lay a basis for other areas to improve on later. All parents need huge amounts of energy at their disposal; parents of children with SEND need superhuman amounts. Every single appointment was a terrifying experience in Sammy's mind. It took unbelievable effort and guile on the part of all adults involved to gain and give any information at all in consultations. This daily reality for specialists and parents is often unremarked. It's frequently an epic, massive victory to ascertain information about the health needs of our children.

I met and saw many other parents dealing with similar issues with their children in clinics, therapy centres, and hospitals as we proceeded through the first decade of Sammy's life. Discussions with these parents and play interaction with their delightful children revealed issues with learning struggles similar to those our own child encountered. There may be many different causes for such children to have difficulty with learning. Quite often, though, similar approaches can help in moving our children on.

Meeting others facing similar challenges can be really helpful. Support groups such as local charities, social services, and self-help forums were invaluable for contact with other families facing similar issues. Adults and children get the chance to connect, support one another, and enjoy activities together. The sheer extra effort and energy spend in raising children with complex needs means that life can be lonely. You may have a child of 6 with the mind of a baby or toddler, which can make socialising both physically cumbersome and socially difficult. All our social meetings, outside of close contacts and similar families, came with a need for explaining strange or inappropriate response or behaviour on the part of our child.

Even at Down's Syndrome Oxford events, Sammy spent the entire party in the foyer for two consecutive Christmases. At least in the second year there was a companion child, also overwhelmed by the sensory experience. They played tag and ate together in the draughty foyer, relieved to be avoiding the noise, colour, and laughter of the party. For our family, it gave a space of acceptance, understanding, and a chance to compare notes on our trials and triumphs. We weren't the only family whose child had run away or had a sudden meltdown because a dog had barked or an emergency vehicle had gone past on the road. Other parents were also having nights of new-born experience, being woken every two hours, and the need to prepare for the routines of each day with a **Social Story,** toy act-out, or **Picture Exchange Communication System**—all techniques we will be exploring in the manual. Many of us had to choose which partner would stop working in order for the other to be free to meet the high-level needs of our children.

The good news? In our peer group, all of our children with Down syndrome or complex needs have made it through most of childhood ... and are moving into the glories of adolescence.

Part Two
Practical Manual of Information

3

Getting Started

Before you begin working through this manual, think about and call in your support. This is a journey best undertaken with helpful, kind people behind you. You will need emotional nourishment, encouragement, and a sounding board for this challenging journey. You may even be fortunate enough to have people who can give you practical help—getting down and dirty, cleaning up, supporting the development of your child's understanding by caring for them whilst you're cleaning up, or giving you hugs, tea, and sympathy. Most loved ones want to help but won't know what you need unless you ask. Give clear and sufficiently detailed direction about your needs.

Turning inward, you will need to accept that you and your child will be outside timings for milestones considered "normal" for child development. You will have to navigate these challenges yourself and support your child to do so. It can feel very lonely and isolating when the rest of the pack at baby groups, nursery, reception class, or school are charging ahead in their development and mastering competencies which seem so far away for your child. Your child not only has the possibility of learning difficulties but is expected also to learn about toileting skills in a society where much of this information is hidden and spoken about only in innuendo and socially coded language.

We live in a society where no one really knows about and therefore can't acknowledge, think about and support those with personal care difficulties. This is the case too for children with learning and development issues. There was scant information about disability and special needs in my training as a teacher. I was in my early thirties and teaching for 12 years before I learned of and thought about the challenge of toileting for disabled people. At that time I taught a delightful student who happened to be in a wheelchair. She told it like it was and lamented that it was not general knowledge. I felt chastened for my own ignorance as a teacher and resulting lack of consideration. A few years later, when informed of my child's diagnosis of Down syndrome, I had no idea about the challenges which lay ahead.

Progress is likely to be slow and in tiny incremental steps. Your child's development in areas such as body maturation, cognitive understanding, and emotional grasp is likely to be much slower than the norm. That's okay. Learning can and does happen for people with learning difficulties, but it is likely to be slow and sometimes halting. There are times when it seems that development is going backwards. You will experience frustration, unmet expectations, exasperation, and despair. This is common to all parents. Your journey, though, is sometimes going to be trying on your nerves in technicolour! You may start feeling months behind contemporaries and end up realising it's more like years. Rather than judge yourself and your child according to so-called norms of development, celebrate what you have and can achieve.

Be kind to yourself. Allow yourself and those who love you to be honest about disappointments and feelings. It's healthy to be honest with yourself when you're ready for it. Your victories, however small, are going to feel epic—the superhero moments you share with your child and will remember forever, your own personal World Cup. There will be lots of these moments as you acquire and apply invaluable insights as you journey forth. Always look for the joy and share it with others. This is your story, and it's going to be great.

Classic Toilet Learning

For all small children, toilet learning requires a huge paradigm shift from a life lived in nappies (or diapers), where elimination of urine and faeces happens freely without the child's attention, and learning when and how a potty should be used. I prefer the term *toilet learning* to toilet "training" as a more accurate description of the child's agency in acquiring this skill.

The time at which children with SEND are ready for toilet learning may occur significantly later than the age when use of a potty is appropriate. Classic toilet learning usually happens between the ages of 18 months and 4 years old. Four is generally perceived as late, but the child is likely still small enough to fit on a large potty. Many children with SEND will have reached an age when their physical size requires learning on a full-sized toilet with adaptations as needed.

But how do you know when your child is ready for toilet learning? The classic guidance is aimed at parents of neuro-typical children.

1. **Look for signs of readiness.** The child is often dry for two hours at a time, is interested in doing things on their own, can pull their pants up and down, can follow one- and two-step directions, and can tell you they need to be dry or clean or behave as if in discomfort.

2. **Move operations to the potty or bathroom.** Change nappies or underwear in the bathroom. Try to work out intervals of nappy soiling and put child on potty at these intervals. Make the potty a fun place to be. Use books, songs, stories, and toys to help child feel relaxed and able to eliminate on the potty.

3. **Celebrate the child's progress.** Make it fun to learn to wipe clean and wash hands.

4. **Dress your child in normal underwear.** The child will learn about the discomfort of soiling and so seek to use the potty to eliminate bodily waste.

5. **Avoid power struggles and negative feelings.** Switch your energy, speech to other activities as soon as possible.

6. All this, of course, is based on establishing and sticking to a routine. It was brilliant advice that worked a treat for our daughter, who was very engaged and able to communicate her needs from an early age. Toilet learning was fast for her and easy for us.

Not so classic toilet learning for a child with SEND.

Your child with SEND is likely to diverge from the classic toilet learning path in a range of ways which are unique to them. Again, throw out timing expectations. It may take a lot of time and effort for you both to master these five steps. It might not be easy. Break it down into smaller steps. Keep going; you'll get there

1. Signs of readiness may never be apparent. You may have dry patches which indicate maturing of evacuation. Or you may not—it will still help to introduce regular intervals for toilet visits. At least you're helping your child to begin on the route to regulation, a skill we all need. Develop your own Picture Exchange Communication System (PECS, pictures with information), role play and comedic modelling. Toys may help. Communicate and give the child a sense of agency. Check out the child's responses and react when they show enthusiasm. Follow up on their positive actions. That's them teaching you what works.

2. Move operations to the bathroom or toilet. It's easier said than done but worth trying to create a toilet routine. You can begin to hurry the harvest by doing this. For sensory needs a routine can be especially important. The whole business of changing rooms and a "pants down, sit on potty" command may be distressing for your child. There can be too many moving parts for the child to cope with.

If it is like a Greek tragedy to get to the bathroom, make the journey fun. Slay some toy dragons or monsters on the way. Make your child the hero of the action. Be cool with the idea that this action may take an age to embed. Remember to celebrate tiny steps. In the classic tales, no hero ever got anywhere quickly. You can make reaching the toilet your Holy Grail—it might well feel like that level of quest at first.

Transition can be a major and difficult deal for some children with SEND. What you do when you get there can be another story. Create fun and comfort there. Work out intervals as best you can. If you can't, introduce a new timing reality and train your child towards it. The essentials are lots of love and positive expectation. The old classics of favourite toys, books and PECS can really help here.

3. Celebrate all achievement, however minimal. If there's a tiny step in the right direction, it's a major goal met. Awareness and willingness to try on the part of the child cannot be assumed. To get to any end point, our children may need to overcome massive internal obstacles.

Constantly model and encourage wiping clean and washing hands. It may be a long time before the child is ready to try. Remember to keep it fun, even if inside you are on your knees. You will be glad you did in the long run.

4. Dress your child in normal underwear *when it works for you both*. This is outside the classic model, but you do need to preserve your relationship and nervous system. Pull-ups can bridge the gap, and reserve the option of soiling normal underwear for home. When we first embarked on this stage, we changed into regular underwear as soon as we got home. This step became a routine rewarded with play or a snack. It gave our child time to learn how to be in normal underpants at his own pace. A child with sensory challenges needs time and regularity to acclimatise to difference around their body and environment. Such a change can be a really big deal for a child with SEND, who may well feel deeply threatened by it. If the change is practised in a familiar, supportive environment, the child receives greater agency and comfort.

When we went cold turkey on underpants, it was with fantastic well-planned support at school. It took a long, long time to get to dry comfort in underpants. Awareness of regularity worked better than discomfort for our child. The discomforted sense developed much later, at a point when a habit of regular visits to the toilet had been established.

5. Avoid power struggles as much as you can. Notice negative feelings and switch energy, speech, and activity as soon as possible. Light and bright is the way to go. Use silly voices, songs, and any fun ideas your child loves.

Although all this is based on establishing and sticking to a routine—again, easier said than done—establish and maintain what you can. Bin words and activities which trigger difficulties. Remember, you're great and doing your best.

4

Diet, Gut, and Psychology

In the early years of parenting my child with complex needs, I wondered if there was some kind of connection between the brain and the gut. I looked around on the internet. I couldn't find much that was applicable to my situation in 2009. Since then a whole new branch of research has bloomed, and a lot of light is being shed on the inside story of our gut-brain connection. Scientists are researching the gut-brain connection and how this operates in children with special needs. Here's what we need to know about the child's gut to help them.

The Enteric Nervous System

The Enteric Nervous System (ENS) which runs throughout our gut and connects directly to the brain is key to overall development in humans, especially small ones with growing bodies. There is a lot to learn from the website Parenting Special Needs (parentingspecialneeds.org). I found an excellent article by Lori Mauer called "The Gut-Brain Connection and Children with Special Needs".[3] Mauer describes a host of symptoms including sleep problems, poor concentration, and diarrhoea, which many parents of children with SEND grapple with.

Mauer explains how the function of gut and brain are closely connected by the neurological system. Deep within the walls of our digestive system lies our ENS, the body's "second brain". The ENS comprises around 100 million nerve cells which line the entire gastrointestinal tract in two thin layers. Mauer argues that the ENS communicates with the brain in a way which may trigger mood changes. She notes sleep problems, irritability, poor concentration, diarrhoea, and trouble with memory as some of the many

---

[3] Lori Mauer, "The Gut-Brain Connection and Children with Special Needs," Parenting Special Needs, https://www.parentingspecialneeds.org/article/gut-brain-connection-special-needs, accessed December 12, 2023.

symptoms that may sign distress along the gut-brain connection. We experienced all of these symptoms for many years in our child's halting development. When I began to be more active about modifying what I thought was an already good diet, I noticed that the tangerines Sammy craved really did help him to regulate bowel and mood function.

It took time and experiments with different foods to work out a suitable diet for our child. The whole effort was greatly enhanced by a diagnosis of MS for me, which got me going on a reappraisal of family meals and to the hedgerow to find diet solutions. It's well known that many modern chemicals used to grow and process our food are toxins. They are often designed to attack the nervous systems of creatures perceived to be "vermin" in twentieth-century agriculture. Not surprisingly, they have a similar cumulative effect on human systems over time, and combining them with the additives in fast foods leads to a toxic cocktail that our children consume in their food.

Nutritionist Kelly Dorfmann's research proposes possible links between poor diet and deficient child development. Dorfmann suggests an epidemic level of development problems among children:

The skyrocketing number of kids with developmental issues cannot help but make a reasonable person wonder if our unchecked use of preservatives, pesticides, genetically modified foods, additives, colorants and other substances is contributing to the epidemic.[4]

Happily, a new mood and movement is emerging in twenty-first century farming in the UK and EU where more care for the environment is leading some farmers and food manufacturers to seek nature-supporting solutions. Governments are also beginning to pledge action. It's my hope that we will see less toxic impact on our future food and drink.

The adage "You are what you eat" rings true. Most of us know when we've caused an imbalance in our system with overindulgence in the wrong food and drink. It's increasingly evident that the junk foods designed for and aimed at children and young people are a danger to their health if overconsumed and not neutralised with a plentiful supply of fresh food such as fruit and vegetables. For many parents, trying to feed healthy foods to their children can be very challenging, but it's worth the effort to persevere.

---

[4] Kelly Dorfmann, *Cure Your Child With Food* (New York: Workman Publishing, 2011, 2020), p. 14.

Improving Ability and Mood

An increasing amount of research about diet points to a link between the child's digestive system and their mood, even mental health. Natasha Campbell McBride, MD, writes in her book, *Gut and Psychology Syndrome*, "It appears that a child's digestive system holds the key to the child's mental development … . The underlying disorder, which can manifest itself in different children with different combinations of symptoms, resides in the gut." Campbell proposes to call this disorder gut and psychology syndrome, or GAP syndrome. "Children with GAP syndrome often fall into the gap, the gap in our medical knowledge."[5]

The rise of interest in and research into the effects of diet on health in children with SEND has resulted in more effective diagnostic tools and guidance. This information is available on the internet and in books which can be bought for a reasonable price. The new understanding of gut activity and links with the wider body gives us parents and carers previously unavailable insight into how we can better feed our youngsters. We know more about how to support their physical, mental, and emotional health and development.

As scientists pay more attention than ever before to the specific benefits and deficits of diet on thought, mood, and behaviour; parents and carers are supported in making diet choices for their families. All parents of young children are familiar with the "sugar rush" which follows consumption of highly calorific processed food. We pay less attention in our culture to the calming supportive benefits of whole unprocessed food for our health and happiness.

Implementing the Right Diet

In *Cure Your Child with Food*, the experienced nutritionist Kelly Dorfmann writes,

What I've studied, witnessed and tested again and again is that nutrition is a way to tweak a child's personal chemistry for optimal health. … In a perfect world … the foundations are simple: whole (fresh, not processed) organic food, lots of fruit and vegetables … . Beyond the basics, most nutritional problems fall into one of two areas: Something being consumed is irritating or something the body needs is missing.[6]

---

[5] Natasha Campbell McBride, *Gut and Psychology Syndrome* (Cambridge: Medinform, 2010), p. 7.
[6] Dorfmann, *Cure Your Child with Food*, p. 12.

Dorfmann proposes a plan for parents to work out systematically which food is a support or impediment to their child's health. She calls this the EAT programme. The acronym is as follows; E- Eliminate any irritants which may be causing a bad reaction. A- Add one food at a time. T-Try one bite of this food each night for two weeks. In this programme, parents and carers are shown how to test whether foods are causing health problems and if so which one. Testing is done through elimination, adding or trying certain identified foods in the child's diet. Dorfmann suggests that parents should persist with a little and often programme of acclimation with different foods.[7]

It's clear we have to find ways to get as much nutritious fresh, organic food as possible into our youngsters as we work out what does and doesn't work. I wish I'd had Dorfmann's wonderful EAT programme at the time we most needed it. Trial and error was our approach over time. Both of our children were picky eaters but they would eat large amounts of pasta sauce and soup in which I was able to hide a lot of healthy stuff with the help of a grater and food processor. Happy days!

We are now largely gluten-free and organic as much as possible This diet has brought noticeable positive results. We eat many foods in their natural state. I rely on batch cooking in large pans to avoid overspend and being permanently stuck in the kitchen. It's an approach which costs more time and energy than relying more on prepacked food, but the payoff is improved family health, as well as children with a taste for fresh food and the beginnings of knowledge and skill about how to prepare it.

---

[7] Dorfmann, *Cure Your Child with Food*, p. 49.

5

The Slower Road: Development Expectations and Patterns

Fasten your seatbelt. Development expectations and patterns are likely to be wildly different from the Neuro-typical path. Physical, mental and emotional development will not be within the usual boundaries. Your child with SEND is likely to need a lot more scaffolded support, explanation, repetition, and assistance with communication than the average child. Repetition is key; opportunities for the child to repeat words and actions will lay the groundwork for development. You will need to find creative ways to go over the same information again and again.

Professional help is available, but it is minimal and can be patchy, as budgets are constrained and competent, caring staff are overwhelmed with large workloads. You are likely to spend a long time on waiting lists. Despite these obstacles, a host of helpful professionals are out there, and local organisations and charities who want to help. Their expertise and assessment will be invaluable. You can improve your understanding and skills around promoting your child's needs. You will need all the assessment, examination, and recording of your child's requirements which is available to you. These services will not only help with accessing health monitoring and support but also provide documentation for underpinning your claim to support for your child.

At the time of writing, only Down syndrome is diagnosed through blood tests. Everyone else has the road of failure in the system and great anxiety before access to support can begin. Nil desperandum, you will get there. Set your mind to expecting support whist you seek it out. Imagine how it will feel. Maintain your will to call it in.

The Plus Side of Parenting and Complex Needs

Your child is wonderfully different to the mainstream. You are now in a place of divergence from the usual expectations, literature, and support.

For children with a whole range of conditions who come under the umbrella of neuro- different and complex needs, the pace of development is much more uneven and delayed than for the average child. All the age-typical milestones are unlikely to be met by your child at the usual times. Milestone reaching is possible, but the timing is likely to take much longer than it does for most children. Comparison is futile.

Your best bet to protect your own strength and emotions is to *embrace* the idea that your path is atypical. To do so will give you more freedom than you imagine. You can get away with the delightful silliness of early childhood for years to come; indeed, the more humour and light-heartedness you can bring to even difficult and awkward situations, the greater your chance of achieving good results.

On the bright side, you're not on the usual trajectory of competition and expectation we subject ourselves and our children to. You're on a different journey to destinations as yet unknown. Welcome the kindness, support, and new perspectives that life will bring. When my child was a baby and struggling on many levels, another mum gave me a huge gift. She said that of her four children, the youngest one, born with Down syndrome, had brought her the most blessings. He had caused her to slow down her busy mind and learn to look, listen, and appreciate in a way she had never done before. She had a thankful heart for the opportunity to spend much longer in and enjoy the different stages of infanthood. This mother became a touchstone for my own heart and mind when parenting became impossibly challenging. Her kind, intelligent words were soothing to recall when dealing with a poonami or the kind of inappropriate behaviour in public in which our child specialised.

Accept with grace, as far as you can, that you and your child are outside timings which are considered "normal". Grace will bring its own magic. Socially, you are likely to meet kind and non-judgemental people who have an instant understanding of and sympathy for your situation because they're there too. Parents and carers of children with SEND can and do form networks. There's a whole world of support and understanding you might not know exists.

Be honest with yourself and others about your expectations. I read in a book that children with Down syndrome make five months development in a good year compared to the twelve months of progress of their Neuro-typical peers. Nobody gave me this advice in a professional context (though in fairness to those busy, often overworked professionals, unless you are with the child on a day-to-day basis yourself, it can be hard to see and chart progress). If your child has additional conditions and health problems, it's necessary to adjust as appropriate.

One friend, a paediatric doctor, was the first professional to be starkly honest with me when my child at age 9 was clearly miles behind peers in development terms. Although every child is different, and we can't truly foresee development prospects for anybody, it would have given us some perspective to know in advance that progress could be so achingly slow.

Your child will make it, but in time with their own growth and understanding. Progression which takes other children weeks and months may take your child years.

Remaining Optimistic

You and your child are on a journey of co-creation. It will sometimes be very tough for you both. Keep reminding yourself that *if they could, they would*. Right now they can't; one day they will.

You are on a superhero journey. Know that the odds sometimes will be stacked against you, but with love, kindness, and grace, you and your child will find a way.

It's OK to panic and to feel alone, bewildered, angry, or embarrassed. That's just body chemistry doing its thing in challenging situations. Try not to feed the negativity with more gloomy thoughts. Have a picture in your mind or a funny thought which is your self-rescue visualisation. I have a beautiful place in Cornwall and a funny family event which happened when I was a child. I feed and talk about these ideas every so often, as if watering a houseplant. It's a mechanism to neutralise my mental negativity, and it works.

I tried and tested it with different classes at school as a thought experiment in PSHE classes. At first, we were exploring the power of self- programming our thoughts to combat exam stress. The idea caught on and spread throughout the school. Some teachers used the approach with form groups, others with exam classes. Older students set up their own informal groups to help with matriculation exams. Those of us among staff and students who stuck to it for a short time reported positive results. We found that thirty days of returning to those thoughts for a moment gave us a habit of positive thinking when facing stressful situations. In my participating classes and with my form group we decided to spend a short time on these focused intentions at the start of sessions. We still felt the stress but were more able to cope, maintain perspective and recover quickly.

You may be wondering, *But how do I give the best help I can to my child with SEND?* Just know that there is life beyond current difficulties for you and your family. To support your child, you will need to be their expert communicator. You will learn from them what works best for them. This is the case for all children, but particularly close attention must be given to children with SEND. They are far more likely to struggle with self-regulation and communication and therefore to find greater struggle in interaction with others.

Teaching Your Child to Learn

Before you can begin to teach anything, you may have to teach your child to learn—to develop the parts of their thinking which seeks motivation and reward. Most humans will do something if they feel an intrinsic need. For people with SEND, that need may have to be created extrinsically by someone else. A child with complex needs may be perfectly happy to maintain the status quo. The youngster may not be aware of or intrinsically looking for a next step. It's your job to put that in place. The child should feel they are in control of the process as far as possible.

You are about to take many tiny steps, often the same steps repeated again and again. Sometimes, maybe oftentimes, you will feel as if you are going backwards. It's like laying tarmac; you are laying down layers of what your child needs to know. We all learn in layers, and that's what your child is doing.

In the following pages, I share techniques to help your child develop the mental underlay for the cognitive carpet. My suggestions are by no means exhaustive. They are simply approaches we found very useful in building our child's capacity to understand and connect with his own body and the world around him. From this point fruitful learning began.

❖ *Make a plan. Remember to keep it simple. Be flexible and adjust where appropriate.*

Breathing

This sounds daft but is an essential thing to pay attention to. As parents and/or carers of children with complex needs, we can be unaware of our own physical responses to the sometimes challenging and often extraordinary circumstances we find ourselves in with our charges. The person you are helping will be tuned into your vibes acutely. These are often people with hyper sensory faculties. If you're feeling negative in any way, their body will automatically respond and function less effectively. We are all transmitters and do better if we are aware of it.

A big, conscious deep breath in and out before you dive into action will assist you and the one you are helping. It's great if you can get your child to do this with you, freeing up two for the price of one, emotionally speaking. If you can choose to say a positive intention for this interaction, all the better. You know which words and manner work for your child. Sammy was amenable to a third party toy using a silly voice as an encouragement. The toy explained that it was breathing up and down. I moved the toy up and down at first to indicate the meaning of the words 'up 'and 'down'. We were learning this at the time. Sammy now joins me regularly for yoga sessions where we breathe up (in) and down (out) as part of our practice. He is now very enthusiastic about yogic breathing. Your soothing words, presence, and humour will go a long way towards meeting your goals of establishing comfort with new ideas and preferred actions..

I know this well because I learned the hard way that negative reactions to the challenge of poonamis just made things worse. It's easy to read or hear this information, but it's very hard to remember it during an unexpected poonami moment. The only way I got to the point of conscious breathing and words was to train myself. It took me quite a while, but I asked everyone around me to support my efforts. Grace was an excellent coach, shouting out, "Mum, remember to breathe and think happy!"

A good place to start is breathing in deeply with the intention of sending away negative thought on the out breath. Control of breath sets a scene and a prevailing feeling for ensuing activity, stopping the negative cortisol and adrenaline build-up before it starts, which is so helpful.

6

Watching, Noticing, Listening: Communication and Cognitive Development

As you support your child, you will become an expert communicator with them. You will be a key person who notices and learns from them what most interests, motivates, and upsets them. This is the case for all children, but particularly close attention must be given to children with SEND, who require extra effort, sensitivity, and emotional intelligence to tune in to their frequency. Speech development is often delayed, if it happens at all. Your job is to establish and support patterns of communication which work for your child.

In working out the best approach for toilet learning, we as parents found that watching, noticing, listening, and communicating were the keys for us in understanding how our child was experiencing and comprehending the world around him. We came to realise that for our child, experience and comprehension were not as closely related as they were in our well-trained adult minds or that of his Neuro-typical younger sister. Tried and tested paths of learning which work well for most had no impact at all. We had to find a way in, a way to glimpse how to connect with his receptors by communicating in various modes in relation to his previous experience.

We listened deeply, checking with him that we understood his communication, watching carefully and moving forwards without our own assumptions and projections getting in the way. I say that; but it is so much easier said than done. We watched our child's interactions with us, other people, and devices such as TV and computers. We also watched out for what he was most enlivened by and what he was trying to get across to us and get from us. We tried different kinds of play, made some notes, had lots of discussions, and tried as best as we could to check out our findings with him in a comfy setting such as the kitchen table—he's very fond of food.

It became clear that he has a highly honed sense of fun and loves cartoon characters with large eyes and animated, exaggerated behaviour. He shouted out at scenes on TV and videos and replayed these situations in play. These interactions gave us an in. We needed something to provoke great engagement and empathy in his thinking to promote our toilet learning aims.

Our teddies, Lego characters, and even Thomas the Tank Engine were soon to play a starring role in our bathroom as champion poo role models. Where our own efforts to model toilet behaviour had failed, our all-star cast of toys succeeded. I even coloured in toilet tissue with brown markers to create a before-and-after effect for our toys to do a poo. Our boy was delighted with this new game, and we slowly began to build with him the idea of using the toilet for a poo. As he instructed his toys about what to do, he began to want to model the behaviour himself.

It took a long time and the employment of many tactics for the penny to drop in our son's thinking. I share some of these tactics in the following chapters.

Strategising

Most of the techniques outlined here will require preparation, practice, and mediation away from the toilet. The name of the game is building cognitive strength and understanding what is portable in your child's thinking. Then you can move those ideas and that understanding into the bathroom. To paraphrase a famous slogan, "Keep it simple, stupid, and repeat it."

Exercise 1: Gather information to create a plan.

Here are some questions to give you a place to start. Your answers here will inform you in making an effective plan for your campaign to assist your child in better toileting. Think of it as your PIT plan—your Poo in the Toilet campaign. Give yourself a month to get started. Make it two weeks if this seems too long and overwhelming.

Observational Questions

Notice your child's behaviour, reach some conclusions, and start to make a plan.

Your PIT Campaign

The goal of planning is to bring your child as near as possible to the destination of independent toileting. You are reading this book because that is not an easy goal to achieve. You already know that you may have to travel with tiny steps. That's fine! You can cover the distance. You will be brave, kind, consistent, observant, and imaginative in carrying out your Poo in the Toilet (PIT) campaign.

Keep a light and bright emotional tone. Remember that toilet training requires a paradigm shift in your child's thinking and action. As your child becomes older, new information will bombard their senses. In addition to physical change and development, your chid will be facing novel situations, settings and circumstances. You may find dips in the rate of their learning. This is common for all children. For children with SEND however, these changes can be confusing and overwhelming. Have faith and patience in guiding your child through. In order to move forward, you will need to help your child develop their thinking skills. The information below can support you in doing this.

- ❖ *You are the chief cheerleader and architect of the social, emotional, cognitive, and physical journey your child with SEND is about to undertake.*

Observational Questions

Notice your child's behaviour, reach some conclusions, and start to make a plan.

1. What does my child like?

2. What does my child like dislike?

3. What does my child want to approach, imitate, touch, or avoid?

approaches	imitates	touches	avoids

Now you have some clues about what will work to motivate your child. The following question is worth careful attention, as encouraging intrinsic motivation for your child will lead to the best outcomes. This is likely to be an ongoing conscious effort. You may be helped by jotting notes and having discussions with others involved with your child. Here lie nuggets of golden information. And if you come up with lots of answers here, great! More tools to work with.

4. What sensory conditions best facilitate my child's learning?

5. What sensory stimuli upset or distract my child ?

6. What do my observations tell me about my child's inner drivers? How is my child motivated?

The barriers to your child's toilet learning may be many, with huge variance among children with SEND. Your child may feel threatened by the toilet or by the room itself. The child may already associate this place with the stress of not understanding what is expected or with a feeling of having failed. ASD, Down syndrome, and other special needs conditions are already tough enough to cope with without the child feeling the imposition of seemingly superhuman expectations. You both may have come to associate this place with difficult effort. People who have neuro-diverse nerves and plumbing are already on the back foot, and we all know the physical effects of negative emotions on our outlook and bodies. Be honest with yourself in answering the question below. It may be painful but it is shedding light on what needs to change.

7a. What are the major barriers my child encounters and experiences when using the toilet?

7b. Under what circumstances do the biggest difficulties occur?

8. Under what circumstances does the child have the best chance of a successful PIT stop?

Exercise 2: Readying your plan for action.

As Shakira sings in her song "Try Everything", there may be several things which just don't work, but eventually something will. You may need to turn detective to figure out the best way forward. I am loath to admit it, but sometimes I was at the top of my own pole with stress and panic in some toileting situations. That certainly didn't help anyone. I had to turn to these questions for myself to detect my own issues here. So be honest here with your answers!

1. What information have I gleaned about stimulating my child's interest and what doesn't work?

2. How can I use this information?

3. What's the first thing I can have a go at trying?

Strategising

No single plan will fit everybody's needs and lifestyle. So before we move on to the Survival Kit part of this book, here's a guided approach to reviewing your observations and laying the groundwork for your own PIT campaign. You can turn almost any answer here to serve your needs. Think imaginatively about how you can use your child's preferences to develop new skills.

First review the steps to toilet learning and identify your child's obstacles. What obstacle do you want to work on first? Then make a list of the things they love. Can you apply any of these to overcome your child's hesitation about this obstacle?

For example, what actions, toys, behaviours and noises enliven and interest your child? How can you build these into your daily PIT routine? In contrast, what does your child normally avoid or reject? How can you make this perceived obstacle more attractive if it's necessary or minimise the impact it has?

It may be that your child struggles with some unavoidable aspect of toilet learning such as the object of the toilet itself or is determined to touch their excrement. Both have happened in my experience with different children. Creating fun distraction, preventing unwanted actions and consistent teaching of new behaviours resolved these issues.

Solutions were developed through identifying drivers for unhelpful behaviour and working out how to remove them. In the first situation where I figured out that the problem with transition to the toilet was fear of the toilet object itself, I noticed the word 'toilet' was a problem for my youngster. Here was a scary and threatening object associated with the feelings of failure already discussed. I worked out new vocabulary and a silly game with toys to play as transition to the toilet. Songs which we noticed he loved from children's programmes or popular music had lyrics adapted by us parents to fit the task in hand. The sillier we became, the funnier Sammy found it. This cheery distraction was built on using a comic voice reward on his arrival upon the toilet. A special, washable toy called Poonicorn was waiting for Sammy's arrival and delighted to see him. Sammy was greeted by Poonicorn in a faux posh military English style. An air of joking silliness was maintained with 'cartoon' voices to keep up the fun distraction. This approach worked well. After the first ten tries, Sammy was looking for the reward of silly voices and initiating the game to travel to places in addition to the lavatory. All kinds of places were greeted with a joke military salute. Other washable toys joined Poonicorn's army. They were familiar, portable, reliable, washable friends which travelled with us everywhere. Once two were left behind by accident at a friend's house where we'd been staying. Our friends posted us a fantastic and imaginative video of Baff (Giraffe) and Key (Monkey) outlining their adventures, including successful visits to the toilet! A linking of our children's loved toys with our overall PIT campaign was invaluable. Thank you our friends, Mol and Zak! In cognitive terms, it contributed a skill called transcendence to Sammy's thinking skills. Transcendence according to Feuerstein, who we will meet later, happens when a learnt idea or concept can be applied in many different situations. This skill is known as generalisation in Educational Psychology and a key thinking goal to reach in school. Sammy could now see, understand and enjoy the idea of him and beloved friends using a toilet with success. This greatly helped with transition issues in other parts of our lives. Regular and entertaining visits to the toilet with toys and singing dissolved the anxiety driving the first problem; fear of the toilet.

Think about how you might link your child's loved things to the toilet tasks you're working on. The examples above show how noticing, planning and serendipity can play a role. If you don't want to sing yourself for example, you could queue up a loved tune or video on your phone to take to the bathroom. This practise certainly helps with ensuring comfort and familiarity when learning a task. Katy Perry's song, 'Roar 'has certainly played a large part to this end in my role as a teacher. Thank you Katy, your work has helped a number of children with special needs achieve more personal independence.

At work, the toilet Learning template for children with SEND outlined earlier in the book was deployed to assist a youngster determined to touch their own faeces. Our goal was to enable toilet learning as far as possible and lessen the compulsion for touching and tasting. Here the driver was a known medical issue, Pica. A person who has this condition feels compelled to taste the objects in their world, whatever those objects may be. Very clear and simple repeated guidance about what to do around toileting using modelling, PECs and contingent touch slowly worked to achieve more independence with personal care. All aspects of the approach were important but arguably contingent touch, repeatedly saying no to and stopping efforts to stick hands near the rectum or in the toilet were the most effective. We achieved a gradual transition away from touching poo. This was done by staff gently holding on to the child's hands during evacuation. A lot of praise was given about the action of pooing in the toilet and contents immediately flushed away. Lots of favourite songs, encouragement and praise were made part of the routine. The non-verbal child could show with sound, movement and expression their enjoyment of the songs and initial annoyance at not being able to touch their poo. We introduced putting hands on the front of thighs as many people do in the lavatory. This behaviour became habitual with repetition. The condition of Pica was not resolved but some self-regulation in personal care became more of a norm.

For the young person, guided experience had to happen regularly before understanding on their part began to form. Poor habits can and should be changed where possible to support personal independence.

Now consider your situation and match your PIT goals to the things you have identified which your child loves. This will assist your aim to remove barriers to their toilet learning. Here are some statements to help you to plan your PIT campaign.

1. I have observed that my child loves …

2. I'm going to use my child's love of _____ to get them interested in overcoming the first PIT obstacle. I can match the two by linking, for example my child's love of a particular song to the activity aim of pulling down pants and sitting on the toilet. We can sing and dance whilst we do this.

3. Before I start to work on my plan, I'm going to share it with my child by sharing pictures, explaining my plan, using Social Stories, and role play. I'll use my child's reactions and wishes to inform how I proceed.

4. I believe my child's obstacles to toilet learning are…

5. The first obstacle to PIT I will work on is

6. I'm going to encourage more comfort in this step forward in toileting by using these tactics…

Before I start to work on my plan, I'm going to share it with my child by sharing pictures, explaining my plan, using Social Stories, and role playing. I'll use my child's reactions and wishes to inform how I proceed. I will encourage and support my child. I will make the toilet an attractive place to be through these behaviours and objects (such as music, props, toys, charts, certificates.) There are resources in this book such as specific **PECS** which you can use. The **PECS** style pictures in this book are ones I created to help my child learn crucial information for toilet learning. I realised that a pictorial representation of the concepts I was using was necessary to help his understanding. He could use the diagrams to communicate his thoughts and sensations. In addition the mystery of what 'poo' and 'wee' actually were began to be clarified using visual language. I talk elsewhere about resources on the internet such as reward charts which you can customise as you need.

Routine Building and Milestones For children with SEND, there is a strong need to build a routine which the child can learn and repeat with comfort. For the child, learning to understand and work within the sequence needed can pose a huge challenge. There are at least 15 parts of the toilet routine which the child needs to master. Each part is a milestone in your child's experience of toilet learning. These 15 parts may be 30 in your child's thinking as other obstacles slow down their comprehension and capacity. It can simply be too much to comprehend the whole task. Here is where milestones come in very handy. Bite size chunks of training often work well. Short, firm but gentle demonstrations and practice work well for most learners. There is a milestone chart at the end of this chapter to help you order your progress. Think of Milestones as accomplishments in themselves. Work your way through at a pace and rate which suits your child. If necessary, please add your own milestones specific to your needs. It is not possible in a format such as this to define and meet goals for every individual. You have a framework however which you can adapt to suit your situation. Finding ways to encourage and reward your child will already be part of your everyday lives. It's likely that you have established techniques which work for you. You can apply those techniques here. You have a new habit for your child to acquire. You are setting up a routine of successful toileting for life.

You are already on the path of Habit Training in many areas for your child. Your goal now is to embed the habits of toilet use in your child's thinking and actions. A toolkit which includes visual instructions and explanations will help. This book contains some tools. There is also a lot of help out there to support you to establish a new routine. The internet is a useful source of printable resources. For example, 'Milestones Autism Resources' at https://www.milestones.org>toilet has a useful training toolkit. The site gives clear guidance and milestones for the toilet use process. There is also the provision of pictures (PECS) to support your child's understanding. The site was founded by two mums of children with Autism. They walk their talk! On the internet there is a host of useful resources for the carer and individual with SEND which are free to use. Helpful websites include; https//raising children.net.au, toileting hygiene. Toilet and https//www.fledglings.org.uk >pages. Toilet training,https://www.milestones.org>toilet. The available sites are always changing so look around. Charities and local organisations around the world share their resources for all. You know that creating your routine is giving your child a key developmental skill. It's worth the investment of your time; giving calm, consistent guidance and support. Your sustained efforts will move your child forwards in building a routine and smashing milestones!

https//www.fledglings.org.uk >pages.toilet training,

https://www.milestones.org>toilet

https//raising children.net.au, toileting hygiene.toilet

Rewards and Praise

You cannot give too much praise. Tools, charts, stickers, treats—it's all 'bribery and corruption' in a good cause. Your child will be stimulated and motivated by huge amounts of positive words about them and their efforts. There is no role here for half-hearted interaction. Your youngster needs a huge amount of beneficial stimulation which bolsters their confidence and self-esteem. Many years of teaching taught me this. Students who felt they were believed in and expected to achieve their best often put in the work, stuck to it, and achieved their goals. Positivity is an underrated aspect of many young lives and shouldn't be. We seem to have developed a societal mistrust of showing appreciation for our youngsters. Then we wonder why so many things go wrong with issues of self-belief and mental health.

There are a lot of generic reward stickers and charts which you can download for free or buy on the internet from sites such as Baker Ross, Twinkl and Amazon. Stationery shops also sell products you can adapt to your preferences. You can choose a design and price which suits you and your child. School may also support you here with materials and ideas. Products are designed to stimulate and interest young users. It is usually possible to match their tastes whether it is unicorns, dinosaurs, vehicles, teddy bears etc. Using blank reward charts allows you to write in your next goal and focuses your child's attention on this precise action. Milestones to chart progress are provided at the end of this chapter but you may need to break information down further into smaller steps and just focus on one thing at a time. Small whiteboards and markers are very useful here. You can quickly make a chart which your child can rub out or pop a sticker on as a sign of development. That one achievement may be a major challenge for your child to reach. Achieving the skill this milestone represents will be a major accomplishment. Well done to you both!

Charting Milestones for PIT stops Here are the major milestones to reach. I'm calling your visits to the toilet PIT stops as part of your Poo in the Toilet Campaign. You may need a lot of time and skill to achieve each one. That's where you will need achievable subheadings!

1. **Get your child to the bathroom**
2. **Enter the Bathroom**
3. **Close the bathroom door**

4. **Pull down clothing**

5. **Sit on the toilet**

6. **Use the toilet**

7. **Get toilet tissue**

8. **Wipe with tissue**

9. **Throw tissue in toilet**

10. **Stand up**

11. **Pull up clothing**

12. **Flush toilet**

13. **Wash hands**

14. **Dry hands**

15. **Leave bathroom**

The chart below is one you can use to track your learner's progress. There are two sections to record the numbers of milestones achieved and those to work on. Use the numbers in the list above to record how you are getting on reaching the milestones.. You can gain insight into patterns of elimination and how this fits with food and drink consumed. This information gives you a clear view of where you are now and what your next actions should be.

My PIT stop Habit Training Milestones

Milestone to achieve	Milestone achieved	Date	Time	W=Wet D=Dry S=Soiled	What happened? U-urinate B-Bowel Movement N-Nothing	My notes

Adjustments and Assessments to make in our PIT campaign. We talked about a paradigm shift in your child's thinking. Toilet learning involves a whole new bunch of concepts and interactions which are very difficult for the child to unpack in their thinking. It is highly likely that issues will arise which you would never have thought of. For example, you may have had a struggle to get or keep your child dressed. Conversely your child may resist the undressing aspect of 'pants down and up' which is necessary to toileting. Clothes and their movement can be very challenging to an individual with sensory needs. Understanding of the societal norms around decency can also be absent. Your aim is to introduce clothing change for a purpose. For the child this can be very confusing! Here we have an example of how one milestone can in actuality involve many components. Each one must be worked through with the child. Below are questions to support you to make adjustments and assessments in your PIT campaign. Use this space to record your efforts and outcomes.

Successes; what worked first and why

What didn't work and why

Adjustments to make

Ideas to try

Moving Forward

Now you have a collection of ideas and observations. You can move forwards with toilet learning with your child. You have thought deeply about barriers to learning for your child and how you can help to overcome them. You have more knowledge about what works best for both of you. The road ahead takes skill as well as some luck, but you've made a real achievement in your lives so far. Look forward to the joys which lie ahead. Remember, what others see as small steps are quantum leaps for your child.

7

Improving Cognitive Ability

An interesting approach to teaching people with SEND is Feuerstein Instrumental Enrichment (FIE) and mediation. Developed by Reuven Feuerstein in the mid-twentieth century, FIE became a fresh way of understanding and meeting the learning needs of neuro-diverse people. Feuerstein and other thinkers in the world of education moved away from traditional top-down curriculum and modes of teaching. They rejected the prevailing assumption that people with special needs were unable to develop their mental and emotional capacities. These educational thinkers believed in the possibility of plasticity in a learner's brain. They worked towards a more pupil-centred and positive method of identifying and playing to the strengths of learners.

This method of engagement with the child highlighted the possibilities for positive change and growth. Feuerstein's belief in the possibilities of cognitive modifiability has since been borne out in countless experiences and much research. The Feuerstein type approach led to the mediation method for teaching people with SEND. I learned about mediation from the educative work of Reuven Feuerstein and the movement based on his practice, the theory of Mediated Learning Experience (MLE).

What Is Mediation?

Mediation comes from the lovely Medieval Latin word *mediare*, which means to be in the middle. As parents and carers, we mediate the world for our children all the time through our explanations and interventions in their life experience. The difference for children with complex needs, however, is that the information has to be delivered in ways youngsters with SEND can digest. It's important to keep things as simple as possible for the child. These young people may not have the cognitive hardware to understand or feel comfortable with the messages given. Our task is to become keenly observant sleuths and find the best ways to reach our child. We stand in the gap, the middle between the child and what is to be learned. Our job is to help them make sense of the information they are receiving. This is how we teach them how to learn. We may have to repeat our mediation many times in different ways before the child can begin to form an understanding. That's fine. Progress can be slow and steady.

Mediation is an approach to teaching and learning, based on the quality of interaction between the leaner (our child) and the teacher (us). Despite drawbacks of disability or neuro-difference, we proceed on the assumption that "the right kind of mediated learning can offer the potential for cognitive change to achieve independence and autonomy."[8]

Mediating Understanding

Mediation is the practice of assisting individual learners to build on what they know in order to change and improve the way they think. The goal also includes the passing on of information. You as the parent or carer are the prime mediator in your child's life.

Mediation involves breaking things down into the smallest parts possible, ensuring understanding and slowly building on that. Parents, carers, and teachers mediate the world to their youngsters all the time. For many children with SEND, a large amount of information, such as the contents of a lesson, concept, or an event, can be just too abstract and overwhelming. The path of interpreting the world on a sensory level is often challenging and even threatening for children with SEND. A gentle and simple approach is always best, if you manage to put it in place. Practise by means of play with toys. Ten minutes a day can be enough to start forming new synapses, the neural pathways in the brain which carry information. We can build new ones by learning new ideas. When your child starts to show recognition in their way of communicating understanding, you know you're ready for the next move.

- ❖ *Keep it simple, keep reinforcing and gradually increase the challenge. Simple, simple, simple.*

Mediation needs to be built into daily life. Your child needs to feel comfortable with the familiarity of your communication methods and encouragement. Even if their reactions are sometimes negative and resistant, find a way to keep going which fits that moment and moves on in a positive way. "Faultless learning" which works well for children with complex needs—no blame is attributed, though it can sometimes feel like a war of attrition for you.

---

[8] Marilyn Dunn Bernstein, Mandia Mentis, and Martene Mentis, *Mediated Learning: Teaching, Tasks, and Tools to Unlock Cognitive Potential* (Thousand Oaks, California: Corwin Press, 2008), p. x.

A lot of your success will come through breakthroughs of understanding outside the classroom and bathroom. The belief underpinning Mediated Learning Experience within the Feuerstein approach is that even people with the least propensity for learning can be helped and structurally encouraged to learn much more. The individual with challenged learning capacity needs a bespoke and structured approach. MLE is what all dedicated parents and carers do naturally; though applying the Feuerstein method systematically requires some degree of training to learn the basics. The method can be endlessly modified to suit the needs of individual learners.

As a serious educational and psychological thinker, Feuerstein developed specific teaching materials called "instruments" to assist the cognitive development of students. The tutor, who is able to more closely understand the student's aptitude and ability, modifies and mediates the instruments with which the learner engages. The approach is predicated on creating a need to learn within the student through subjects and questions which cause interest and challenge. As the student engages in the activity, existing neural networks in their brain are fired and new ones created. The student is able to master information and patterns of thinking which improve their mental capacity.

There is a Feuerstein Institute in Jerusalem and other centres around the world. Our son attended the centre in Jerusalem for three weeks, where he and I were given some special training. I had already attended the basic week-long training in the UK, which gave me a good grounding in how to approach the task of mediation for my child. This was the point in our learning journey where we first saw a real development of understanding for him. He began to grasp abstract concepts like time, position, space, and emotion. The instruments designed to address and enable this understanding were invaluable for my son and for other children I have worked with in schools. You can find information online about the various Feuerstein centres around the world and how to find training.

Putting the Feuerstein Approach into Practice

Children with SEND do not always learn the underlying basics in the usual flow of life. From infancy to kindergarten, when understanding of these concepts is being developed among their Neuro-typical peers, the child with SEND thinking may be grappling with a difficult medical or social situation, and their thinking has not developed to understand life in the same way. The mediated approach begins at the simplest possible level to engage and then challenge the child's thinking. A good example of the FIE method is the instrument based on the concept of parallel lines. This is part of a series of FIF tools called, 'Organisation of Dots'. The student watches the mediator draw two parallel lines on an A4 whiteboard and copies this on their own whiteboard. The learner then repeats this activity until the mediator is confident that the concept is grasped. Hands and arms can also show parallel lines. The embedding of the concept begins with the student using a FIE instrument where the child looks for and locates possibilities for drawing parallel lines among a sea of seemingly random dots on a printed, laminated page. The child follows a prescribed pattern and method to do this work, looking for useful information in the patterns between the dots. The student then draws their lines on the page and is encouraged to notice what they are finding out. This is teaching cognitive discipline which can be applied to other learning situations. The student is carefully guided by a mediator throughout the process and as much language and communication as possible is stimulated. There is no right and wrong way for the student to approach the task. Trial and error is an important learning technique. When the child has understood and learned the concept or topic under study, the reasoning is extended further. A distinct and purposeful link is made with a wider understanding of the world around. For instance, the child studying parallel lines will be encouraged to find parallel lines in the room around them to strengthen and embed the concept in their thinking. The act of applying recent learning to the world around us is called 'transcendence' by Feuerstein. The student is able to generalise and apply their new thinking skill to everyday life. All stages of the method trigger a particular type of thought in the student's brain. This is where the brain training happens. The learning is purposely designed to scale out from the small, scant and particular detail to a larger range containing more information. A concrete task is used to underpin the learning of an abstract concept. Feuerstein refers to this as "transcendence". A mind which has reached transcendence can take these concepts and apply them anywhere.

I was part of a research team using the Feuerstein method. We all found surprising and positive results with our learners with SEND. Much of the Feuerstein material is and can be introduced to the child in the format of a game. Within a couple of sessions, it will be clear to the tutor/mediator what aspects of cognitive ability and learning need to be developed in the student.

As an example, one child I worked with, who had a diagnosis of Down syndrome and ADHD, became very impatient and angry if asked to stop and think about the tasks. This characteristic was interrupting all his learning. He could not organise his attention, thoughts, or emotions long enough to absorb and act upon information. We were working on an instrument called Organisation of Dots which can be used at different levels to meet and extend a learner's capacity. The practice involved can be applied as well to all kinds of activities which require forethought and application, to advance cognition and emotional self-regulation. With this particular child, I found that time, patience, and effort on both our parts were necessary. We attained our goals of him being able to focus, consider his options, and work on the task in hand. Planning and execution of task, based on self-regulation, was a difficult skill for him to attain, but he got there. Repetition, encouragement, and a negotiated reward helped. Once the child experienced, developed, and could deploy self-discipline, his will and capacity to engage in learning improved.

Use of the Organisation of Dots instrument helped this individual to identify and overcome several barriers to learning which had held back his development. He gradually became able to accept that his need to rush through all work left him without the benefit of learning the content. It was hard for him to learn to relax and concentrate, but he learned these skills and was surprised at the positive change it brought in learning and relationships.

Another individual was loath to apply any effort from the get-go. He was so afraid of trying that he had no concept of how achievement might feel. He had never got that far. When tasks were simplified and a faultless learning approach was applied, he gradually became motivated to achieve more. His success fed his willingness to continue. He acquired an implicit need to learn.

These are just two examples of success achieved through using Mediated Learning Experience. I have seen significant development in different children's capacities using MLE, including emotional as well as intellectual development. Developing emotional intelligence can be a real point of difficulty for many children.

Different children can encounter many barriers to learning which are not always easy to detect. Unhelpful patterns of thinking can be embedded from an early age, or health and social issues may cause problems we can't see. Mental health issues may manifest in aggression and poor behaviour. Many conditions and situations can lead to social and learning difficulties.

For example, whilst I was working with one individual on emotional instruments, it became clear that he had no understanding of the meaning behind facial expressions. He was shocked to learn about the information codes we express through the faces we pull. This individual had withdrawn himself emotionally from his family at a difficult time for them. He was a toddler then, at the age when we are learning these codes as a part of everyday life. He had simply missed out on learning how we connect emotionally using facial and body language. He had spent a childhood misreading signals and situations. He found himself acting inappropriately in many settings and was viewed as difficult.

His delight in learning the codes hidden in facial expressions was inspiring. We practised identifying emotions in pictures and learning the art of inferring information from body language. Our transcending homework was to pull different faces showing different emotions and to compare results. We both benefitted from our work together. It was a delight to see transformation in his relationships and behaviour as he applied his new understanding. His approach towards school changed dramatically for the better, and he made meaningful friendships for the first time.

It can be very hard for teachers, engaged with large classes and many learning needs, to make time and space for detailed focus on one individual in class. As parents and carers, we can support our youngsters and teachers by doing some of the groundwork at home. Speak with school staff about your ideas and actions. You'll find it works well for everybody. You may well find positive improvements in your child's motivation, ability to communicate, engagement, and language development.

Other Ways to Mediate

The Feuerstein approach is not the only way to introduce a mediated challenge into your child's learning. We found the experience excellent, but it was expensive. There are many other possibilities for developing and enriching your child's cognitive capacities which are more affordable. For example, in our experience, games by a company called Smart Games were effective for our child and challenged our own thinking too. Begin at the easiest levels and be prepared to be fully involved. You will soon work out what level your child is at and what kind of abilities they need to develop next.

Our child's favourite game is called Camelot Junior. It is a game with physical wooden parts of specific size and function which can be used interchangeably. The player has to figure out how to use the blocks to build a bridge between the prince and princess at opposite ends of a castle. There are many games and answers are not obvious unless you've developed the necessary thinking skills. The child has to try different ways of finding a solution to join the royal couple. It gave us the opportunity to extend language development in a fun way whilst doing some serious problem solving. Games which are predicated on finding solutions to tricky problems really encouraged our son's brain to stretch and grow. He was motivated to extend himself and try to solve the problems.

In addition to creating a need to learn in the child, a super large amount of praise and encouragement is needed. It's all about brain chemistry—you're going for the dopamine reward connected with that activity. The "happy chemical" dopamine is released when a person feels good about something. Most youngsters love play. Our aim is to further mental understanding and link it to feeling good, making play an effective way to teach.

Sharing Ideas

Any suggestions you find in this book are by no means exhaustive. They are simply approaches we found very useful in building Sammy's capacity to understand and connect with the world around him. Experiment with ideas you come across, and share them with others. We learn so much through sharing our ideas. Below are some techniques which worked really well for us in building our child's mental underlay. He needed the base layer of understanding before formal school learning could work for him.

Understanding the relationship between things can open up a whole range of concepts which may not yet have developed in your child's mind. This can be as seemingly simple as fitting a toy car in a box garage or seating a toy person in the car and having them drive it. We assume that the concepts of space, placement, language, and direction involved in this transaction develop naturally in children's understanding. Sometimes for a child with SEND they just don't. Concepts such as inside, outside, on, above, up, down, below and towards can be just meaningless words. Concrete examples of these concepts may have to be repeatedly taught and the child engaged in meaningful learning interaction about them. There are a plethora of opportunities in daily life to practice these concepts. Putting objects in and taking them from boxes and drawers are simple examples. Placing objects in, on and next to others with your enthusiastic commentary builds grasp of abstract concepts. Use your imagination to expand and explore possibilities for learning. Walking, cycling and driving either for play or in real life build understanding of these abstract concepts. Point out these ideas and encourage your child to demonstrate and verbalise them. Build up your child's comprehension of these words at a simple, practical level. Young children and many older ones with SEND need concrete physical examples to create understanding. Stimulate building of new synapses in the learner's brain by encouraging their physical involvement in moving objects around and identifying their position. This can include them positioning their whole body for example, in and out of a room, lifting hands and legs and other play possibilities. You are tuning into the body's neural network. Physical movement increases the chances of programming in the new ideas. Your interaction will guide you in what to do and show you where the problems are in the learner's perception and understanding.

As noted, relative concepts about space and time expressed in small words such as *in*, *on*, *next to*, *with*, *now*, *later*, *until*, *before*, *to*, and *from* can be especially tricky for people with SEND. Games or playing with objects such as toys and household objects can help explore these concepts and meaningfully improve comprehension and confidence. You can model meaning and build mental capacity. Try asking the child to follow a simple instruction using a phrase such as "from [this place] to [this place]". Here you can move a spoon from one part of a worktop to another. The concept of place and space is involved but the action is simple. You can gradually build complexity by adding more place points. You can also ask the child to verbalise the instruction or to instruct you using language, gesture (hand, head, eye movement), or whatever capacity they've got. It sounds very simple. The chances are that you went past that point in your own development so long ago that you can't remember doing it. Remember these things aren't always obvious to a child with SEND. *Keep it simple* until you're sure a particular skill is mastered by your child, and then you can build on it. The child needs to feel confident in whatever communication capacity they have before they can learn more.

By "building", I mean adding more information and tasks one step at a time, checking your child's understanding consistently. Build confidence by giving them the opportunity to show off about their new ability. Try pretending to make mistakes at something they know how to do. They will delight in showing you how to get it right. Giving your child the power to correct you builds the confidence and agency you are aiming for. That is when your child becomes transcendent, as Feuerstein would say, putting their new skills into action. The thought of this still overwhelms me with joy. Your progress will depend on the child's engagement and ability, but getting further is always possible.

Build the underlay of your child's thinking by making it fun. Your mediation should be fun, simple, and repetitive. Communicate actively and enthusiastically with your child to build understanding of the basics. Neuro-typical children just pick up these essentials in day-to-day communication and peer play. Our young children with SEND don't yet have this capacity, so basics pass them by and deepen their sense of mystification about the world. Conversely, almost any activity can become a mediation pursuit. Always stay near to your child's capacity and understanding, and then build from there. You're aiming for a small, achievable challenge which the child is ready to think through.

Concrete Examples of Mediating

One example of mediation about emotions would be to point out a picture of a person in a magazine, book, newspaper, or screen who is exhibiting an emotion, and then ask the child what they see. Their response, or lack of it, will inform you about their perception of the stimulus. You can then support the child's response by remarking on an aspect of the picture and asking open questions to enlarge the answers you've received from your child. If the child is non-verbal, you can establish signals for yes/no/maybe. Point to aspects of the picture and ask questions which the child can answer using these visual signals. It's usually easiest to start with the positive. Pick a picture of a person smiling. Ask questions like, " Is this person feeling happy?" "How do you know that?" "Point to the part of the picture which shows the person is feeling happy?" "Why do you think this person is feeling happy?" "Please show me how your face looks when you're feeling happy" Remember to be super encouraging and heap on the praise. Notice how the questions keep mentioning the word 'feeling'. You are laying down the vocabulary and concept of emotions. Understanding motions can be a minefield for people with SEND. Comprehension and expression are frequently difficult.

To simplify; if your child isn't ready, try pulling faces like the one in the picture and asking what emotion you are showing. Then ask the child to pull the same face as you to start with. Here you are making a link in the child's understanding about the emotional meaning behind facial expressions. You can then elaborate further and ask how the person in the picture feels. You then have options to explore and deepen understanding about emotion. You can talk about feeling happy, sad, bored, angry, surprised, or any other emotions. You can find pictures of these emotions, practise pulling and guessing mood faces, and talk about why these moods might be occurring. You can open up the discussion to a wider understanding or notes of transcendence by asking your child about situations in their life where these feelings occur. You can strengthen the child's sense of empathy by exploring where people in their lives show these feelings. Your communication and interaction with your child will speak volumes about their level of understanding.

Next you could extend understanding by asking about the concept of place. "Where is the person? Why do you think they are there? What do you think they are feeling? Why are they feeling that way?" This gives you and the child the opportunity to explore which emotions can be seen or inferred. The latter is often a very difficult skill for people with ASD. If you can gradually support a move to a more cogent understanding of emotional expression, you are supporting the child to gain more comfort and control in their own mind and body. In my experience, teaching about emotion and recognising the different feelings and what may trigger them has been vital.

The area of social and emotional learning is tricky for many children for hosts of reasons. It's a minefield for children with SEND, and an ongoing area of development for our child. Puberty is changing many goal posts with a consequent need to revisit and build upon emotional understanding work from the past. Compared to younger days, Sammy has more thinking and emotional tools with which to widen his field.

Research with young people of all abilities highlights the need for very clear emotional education if one is to navigate oneself and life successfully. Expanding your child's emotional understanding and repertoire of self-expression is invaluable. Life is full of chances to do so. You can use a whole family meal to have a simple game of mood guessing from faces pulled around the table, and then extend identification to mediation on why someone may be feeling a particular way that includes everyone. A visiting guest may provide an even more broadening experience because the child has to deal socially with emotions and information sharing within the group. If the emotional learning is embedded in the child's familiar environment, the chances of deep learning are so much greater.

- ❖ *Mediation is building a bridge of understanding your child can cross to learn about the world. You are the architect, technician, builder, and guide.*

8

Improving Communication

The ability to communicate effectively is a key skill for us all. Children with SEND can have one or more specific physical and learning difficulty which seriously limits their ability to communicate clearly. These difficulties may manifest in similar ways although diagnoses are different. Speech delay is commonplace, struggles to understand the messages and intentions of others occur frequently. The reasons behind the problem can be cognitive, physical, and emotional or all of these. Behaviours exhibiting fear and panic in response to certain stimuli or none are often seen. I have encountered too many difficulties with communication to list in this introductory paragraph. I have also experienced watching children with SEND improve their capacity to communicate and in some cases transform their experience of relating to others. Communication is a key part of socialisation. For you as a parent or carer, efforts to reach out to others experiencing similar issues with their family can provide important social support and a setting and peers for your child. Speech and language difficulties are common in this group. In many developed countries there is a right in law to consult with a speech and language therapist, a SALT. A SALT will be able to assess your child's abilities and suggest activities to address their needs. You as a parent or carer can have a very positive impact on supporting your child to communicate if you learn and put into regular practise the steps which are needed. I had an A4 note book which I took to Sammy's many appointments. I wrote down all useful suggestions and used them to make a plan. I shared these ideas with family, friends and educators to ensure consistency of message and encouragement in Sammy's experience of communication. That way, he was given clear messages and all his support was connected. It's important to have some clear targets, key skills, words and signs to focus on at any one time. Too much information will be confusing for your child. Do feel empowered to ask questions even if you feel stupid to do so. This is a chance for you to learn what you need to know to help your child. Everyone wants the best for the child's development. Professionals in your local medical and educational services can suggest and signpost possible options of support where you live. There is also a lot of information available in literature, journals and on the internet. Local neighbourhood groups can also be useful. Keep asking and looking. You will find people who share your issues and those who can help.

There are many ways to improve your child's capacity to communicate. Here are some I've found helpful.

Makaton Sign Language

Makaton is a language programme which uses hand signing alongside speech and symbols. It is deliberately close to the gestures we use naturally in speaking English. This fantastic technique gave us the freedom to communicate long before our child could develop speech, which is still minimal for him at 13 years old. Makaton really helps when a child can't communicate and is frustrated about trying to get their message across. You don't need much to start with. The capacity to communicate basics such as *food*, *wash*, *toilet*, *TV* or *tablet*, *like*, and *dislike* gives your child the power of agency in the world. Materials and courses can be found on the Makaton Charity website. Often there's a link or provision local support groups can recommend. Look for a class near you.

Makaton can give your child a voice and the opportunity to join in conversations and enrich understanding. There is an emotional benefit, too, which makes life much easier. Our child loved having a secret language—it really suited his mischievous nature!

PECS

The Picture Exchange Communication System (PECS) is a type of augmentative and alternative communication using pictures or visual symbols to communicate information to a leaner or user. PECS are widely used in educational and therapeutic settings to support children with SEND. PECS look like simple, easily understood cartoon like representations of particular words. Education staff download, print and laminate the symbols to use or display as needed. The symbols are then put for example, on cards which the user can deploy in many different ways. Children have PECS timetables showing the sequence of the day's activities and bespoke PECS books which perform as their communication tool. The child can show you a picture of their need or request and understand the reply in PECS's language. They are frequently used in special and many primary schools in the UK. The easily recognisable symbols of PECS teach and allow functional communication. They give additional clarity and security to learners with regard to activities in the day. Only trial and error can tell you whether they will work in your situation.

We used PECS for many areas of life in which our child struggled. We used PECS with pictures and PECS with simple words on. All the pictures are clear and simple in meaning. The PECS also helped us communicate what we were doing now and next. (We made our own "now" and "next" PECS as a trial to begin. I just used card and felt pen stuck with Blu Tac on the kitchen wall).We could communicate our next move, e.g. *walk to school, toilet, meal*. The PECS for communicating time, now and next were aligned vertically so the "now" card could be removed by the child as soon as that activity was finished. The trial worked and we decided to work with PECS. We were helped by our wonderful Speech and Language Therapist, (SALT) who made us a set of PECS cards and later I found and bought them on the internet. We used Velcro bought in a craft shop to stick male and female Velcro tabs on our PECS cards and the boards they were attached to. They were kept in an easily reachable place at home with a Velcro board so our child could communicate his wishes to us too. For a non-verbal child grappling with a complex condition, PECs have offered a new way of understanding the world. Sammy's understanding of some difficult concepts has advanced hugely. This communication method offers him surety about being understood. Sammy developed the skill to conceptualise his day using PECS and Social Stories. At the start of the day, the order of the day was on the wall in PECS vertically. We started with a small step routine; waking up, having breakfast and a drink, brushing teeth, wash, dressing etc. The routine and vocabulary were constantly and securely embedded in his thinking. He liked to say, "Check" to each item on the wall chart as he tore it off before he set off for school. The new level of information he understood was a game changer. We could now work with the abstract concept of times during a day which we later built into longer periods. This is still a work in progress. Weeks, Months and Years are our present work. We never needed PECS in the after school period where he was calmer but still in routine. Sammy began to control his time for the next day by setting up his PECS morning timetable. His school did something very similar to assist his understanding of his day and order of activities. Sammy became less anxious. This freed up time and energy for other learning and fun activities. These are described elsewhere in this book. We regularly furthered our child's understanding of time by looking forward and back at ordering the events of the day. Sammy was learning to conceptualise his day. Building synapses and deepening connections in his brain was the aim here. Sammy began to grow confident with language using his PECS. He now uses spoken bits of language for all the information which PECS provided. This instant visual aid was invaluable in helping him develop his grasp of language and deeper abstract concepts. We no longer need or use PECS. I recently gave away our PECS cards, information strips and boards to a family in need similar to ours a few years ago.

Visual support such as PECS and Makaton Communication help your child to understand what is happening and what they are being asked to do. Several charities and public bodies offer materials and guidance about PECS. Free printable PECS materials are available on the internet and can also be found on the website, 'National Autism Resources' based in the UK. The resources in this book include my own version of PECS for the very specific tasks of toilet training.

Body Part Awareness

Teach body parts as early as you can. Make it a game whenever possible so the information is light and fun to learn. The more positive the child's emotions, the more easily the information is taken in and remembered in mind and body. Here are some examples.

Body Part Games

Work round all the body parts and what you use them for.

> "Where is your nose?"
> "Am I touching my arm?"
> "Can you help me find my chin?"
> "What do I use my eye for?"

When this game is established and your child recognises the main body parts, you can move to the bottom and talk about poo.

It will be a matter of personal choice, of course, as to how you model your own toilet behaviours to your child. The more natural, matter of fact, and positive you are about your own toileting, the more emotionally secure you are setting your child up to be.

Toy Friends

The body parts game also can be used with toys outside the toilet to develop understanding about the body. Children with challenged nervous systems will benefit from "friends" for comfort and support in learning about life's mysteries.

We made sure all our toilet friends were washable. Three main toys gave us toilet time support, so that one could always be in the wash. If one of the toilet friends got messy, we just said, "Oh dear, time for wash." Our toilet teddies became masters at pooing out coloured-in toilet paper as demonstrations. Grace, Sammy's wonderful sister helped me colour in white toilet tissue with big brown marker pens. We tried to make it look realistic and had a lot of colouring in to do! We stashed the brown rolls in the toilet cupboard and made sure we sneaked a few pieces in for demonstration visits. Sometimes we have to stoop to conquer!

The Squeeze Game

We need to squeeze our abdominal and rectal muscles to have a poo. It's not obvious to a child with SEND what squeezing a muscle is. Helping Sammy learn to squeeze his muscles was a challenge. Sammy had the triple obstacles of weak muscles due to Down syndrome, lack of body awareness thanks to his autism and no idea about what squeezing was. It was another situation where he pulled a face to copy us but with no awareness of what the word, 'squeeze' meant. For our boy, learning to squeeze things was a challenge at first. We built squeeze action into daily life and then to parts of our body. From ketchup to toothpaste and wringing out wet clothes after wet play, it's amazing how much squeezing we do. We did a similar thing with pushing. This was easier for us to teach and Sammy to grasp.

We began with learning to squeeze body parts we knew he was already aware of: "Can you squeeze your hand?" or face, tummy, and so on. Once this concept and action is established, you can ask the child if they can squeeze and push on the toilet. Encouraging our child to squeeze his bottom was a game changer in encouraging his awareness and muscle memory for toileting

Yoga

Forget mysticism—yoga can have some very practical applications. Yoga can be a tool to increase body awareness and strength. This can be practised outside the bathroom. Yoga is about moving energy round the body. There are many types of yoga which can be deeply practical as well as spiritual. Sammy and I learned a new type of Yoga in Jerusalem which has been designed to assist people with SEND. This style seems to aim at connecting deep physical memory with mental, emotional and spiritual processes. We laughed a lot with our teacher as we learned this method. We still use it sometimes though Sammy now joins me often in my Kundalini Yoga practise. The following information is a precis of what we learned and you can adapt these ideas to suit your needs.

Rub and sing about a part of your body: "This is my arm," "This is my tummy," "This is my bottom." Encourage your child to imitate you. Make it fun and simple to do. Touching and rubbing the body along with song and chant are an aspect of some yoga practice. Yoga is about body awareness and opening the energy flow of the body's systems. This works especially well for children. For example, once the child knows what the tummy is and develops an awareness of feelings in their tummy, they can begin to sense and share what their physical feelings and needs are.

You can extend yoga to exploring how parts of the body feel: "My body feels happy and ready for the loo." Put in the words and language you need to develop. You can use PECS cards here to give your child a voice and a choice with what they want to say. The child may have feelings which are not so happy and these can be explored too. My PECS can help here.

Songs and Musical Instruments

Make these fun and inclusive. Shake it up and bang or clang your new way forward. You can use existing tunes and add your own words which fit your child's vocabulary and understanding. Another route is to make up your own songs. Be a child again yourself and see what words you can get to rhyme, fit your aims, and lift your mood. Here's one we used.

> Ooh. I need a poo-ooh,
> And I'll do it in the loo.
> I feel so good right through!
> Ooh, I'm pooing in the loo.
>
> Ooh, I did a poo;
> I did it in the loo.
> There is my lovely poo
> Which I did in the loo.
>
> I'm a clever boy; [or I'm a clever girl,]
> I did it with my toy [the best one in the world].

Our son couldn't produce many words but he moved his fingers to the beat of the song to show his appreciation of the tune. Eventually he could make the L sound for "loo" and say "poo", which was great for us.

Sammy got off the toilet one day, said,"Stoi here" and disappeared. I waited for a few seconds and he returned with toy musical instruments from a box in the living room. He decided to introduce musical instruments into the occasion. This helped with bowel clearance when he was blowing a plastic flute or trumpet. Shakers were not such a physical aide but added to the fun element of learning this skill. We soon had a percussive musical routine using drums for getting to the toilet and then a lot of help from the wind and brass section. Instruments which are blown are excellent for creating the pressure or squeezing for bowel clearance. It was great that this was Sammy's idea and it really helped..

Rewarding Body Awareness Progress

Of course, the ultimate aim is toileting independence. So when you do achieve any small milestones on the road to regular supported poos, other tools such as reward charts and stickers can come into play. These tools can of course be useful earlier in the process for targets such as getting your child to the toilet and remaining seated. This was a challenge for our child who even at a young age had mastered the art of quantum gravity, becoming too rigid and heavy to move. He had been traumatised by a lot of necessary medical intervention in his early years and did not want any kind of interference around his body. It took long, gentle, and painstaking effort to build his confidence around being helped and to surrender to his bodily needs. He responded positively to stickers and reward charts as positive motivations to learning.

Once you know what works, the child can then be encouraged to improve their pooing skill and other abilities such as independent use of toilet tissue and washing hands. This may all take as long as it does but with lots of engagement and encouragement, you may find your youngster is becoming more confident and empowered.

9

Toileting and Poo-Specific Mediation: Timings and Action I Need to Establish for PIT

You will need to establish timings and action which support your child's toilet learning. You need to work out the best times to put your child on the potty or toilet. You will also develop an understanding of the best actions you can take. Your needs will be dictated by the level of your child's understanding and development. For example, your child needs to learn the difference between wee and poo. This something you are required to teach. The actions you take will be governed by your understanding of the child's needs and abilities. Sammy did not have any sensation of poo leaving his body. We didn't know if and how he experienced the need to go to poo. In the early days of trying, there was no amount of our communication about it which seemed to impact his understanding. At this point, he had just started to master going for a wee. He had the sensation and, being a boy, could see the action. But for years he called a wee a "poo" because this word had lodged in his thinking. Even if he was using the wrong label, we went with it following the faultless learning approach, which is encouraged for children with Down syndrome. Faultless learning does not seek to correct mistakes instantly. The child's engagement with the subject is to be encouraged above all other factors. Any effort in the right direction should be praised. Adjustments in understanding and modifications can be built into the learning process later.

As toilet-teaching parents, we observed and worked out roughly the timing between food and poo. Within a couple of weeks, we were able to gauge more accurately when to ask our son to get on the toilet. About two hours after a meal we commenced toilet visits at thirty minute intervals. We made sure that every thirty minutes, we popped him on the toilet—not the potty, as he was way too big. The thirty-minute effort soon became too much. Eventually we began operating on two-hour intervals between toilet visits. These were more natural and manageable. The constancy of this practice engendered a habit of regular visits to the toilet in our child's own thinking and habits. Breakthroughs began to occur.

Poos were being deposited in the toilet. I still hear the "Hallelujah" chorus" from Handel's *Messiah* when I recall these early moments of triumph.

We eventually figured out the timings for toileting which were most appropriate for a poo, and we modelled our own toilet behaviours with encouragement and praise when our son began to show an interest in trying to do things his own way. Below are some materials to help you work out your own timings and action.

The Child's Understanding of PIT

The first time our child did a poo in the toilet, we didn't think he had a real intention because we had just happened to pop him on there at the right time. He seemed genuinely puzzled about our elation. The huge breakthrough for us all was the first time our child did a poo on the toilet when he had chosen to go there himself because he had a feeling in his "ummy". We did a lot of cheering and congratulating whilst the longed-for creation sat in the loo. Our son was delighted at our elation, but it took some time for him to realise how to connect the dots in his own thinking. At first, he was happy because we were happy with him. He hadn't really felt the poo, it seemed, nor had much awareness of it other than the feeling in his tummy. We continued with our practices and routines, carefully repeating the information and eliciting a response in slightly different but familiar ways. We reassured our child with familiar terms he liked. We sought to stretch our child's routine and capacity to imagine more and go further in understanding. We asked family and friends to praise his achievement. Our wonderful support team, Sophia and Seren, were warm, enthusiastic champions of his efforts. It was a wonderful experience to watch our son's grasp of this essential life skill become a new competence. He was consciously performing his brand-new skill. News travelled fast. Distant family and friends rang, emailed, or messaged to pass on congratulations. He had reached this milestone at ten years old. Our boy was made to feel like a world champion and rewarded with great praise and, for once, too much of the wrong food. He celebrated himself, sensing if not knowing for sure at that point that something amazing had been achieved in his life.

Techniques Which Work: Pit Timings

Observe the wee and poo habits of your child. Knowing intervals at which they wee or poo will help you form a plan for encouraging PIT stops. You may wish to keep a "wee and poo" journal for a period of time. Below are some questions which are useful to ask.

1. How often does my child need to wee? When does my child poo in relation to meals? In the morning, afternoon, or evening?

2. To begin, I will take my child to the toilet every ___ minutes/hours during the day. I will adjust these intervals as needed. I will also take note about the relation of wee and poo. What happens at which intervals? Are bladder and bowel functions related for your child?

Part Three
Survival Kit

In Part Three, I've gathered some materials and suggestions to support toilet learning. I hope you will think of this part of the book as your survival kit for your superhero journey. There's one for you, and one especially for your child. These are to be read, reread, and used for practical, emotional, and psychological support. Choose the parts which work for you. The process of toilet learning can be long and sometimes very frustrating. The survival kit for your child will most likely need to be read by you and other assisting adults. Encourage your child to look at and read the material here as far as they are able. If necessary, read the information to the child. It's important that a sense of ownership is built up by your child as part of their PIT campaign. The aim of the game is empowerment for your child.

You may find that you would like to keep a copy of some strategies on hand. I encourage you to photo copy these sections and laminate them so they can be wiped clean easily. You have your own set of **Ten Commandments** in this chapter. This is a checklist for your toilet teaching survival which can be printed, laminated, and taken into the bathroom to support you. The child has their own copy of **PIT Stop Checklist** so they can both imitate your action and have their own kit which you can read to them. If your child cannot read at all; that's' no problem. The point here is that your child feels ownership of their own **PIT Stop Checklist** and they are copying you, the carer. I made lists with my son, and he loved saying, "check" when we completed some reading or an action. The Ten Commandments and **PIT Stop Checklist** here are loosely based on this idea. It relieves the stress experienced by children with ASD when they are the focus of attention. Some people with SEND conditions struggle with being the object of attention. **The PIT Stop Checklist can** become the subject rather than the child. This gives the youngster more comfort. We found this diversion very helpful. We minimised oversensitivity to direct attention. **The PIT Stop Checklist Idea**s later in this section outline ideas for engagement and activities which the child can use to support their understanding and willingness to engage with the task in hand.

You'll also find a questionnaire to support making a plan which is bespoke for the needs of your child. It includes questions which probe for the information you seek and connects to mediation preparation. On various sites on the internet, as noted in chapter 6, you can easily find and print off reward and sticker charts. Use these to mark and celebrate your child's steps towards and achievement of the goals you set. Aim to be interactive and encouraging for the child. Try to create a sense of fun, positivity, and achievement around all things connected with toileting. This book contains PECS style diagrams showing different emotions and actions linked to toilet learning. These are more graphic than regular PECS in showing detail for example about how wee and poo look when they're happening. Some diagrams of emotions we used are also included.

Children with complex SEND conditions are unlikely to develop an understanding of their place in the world alone. This survival kit aims to provide you with some essential tools for your thinking and practice. It includes techniques and materials that you as a /parent or carer can acquire and put in place. Photocopy as much of this book as you need. Customise and reuse as you see fit.

So I leave you with this thought.

- ❖ *Your child can develop the understanding and skills of toilet learning and learn other things. It just takes longer, and you're their best teacher.*

To the Parent or Carer

Dear parent or carer,

You know the spiky profile of development in all children is particularly accentuated in children with SEND. We all have different gifts and difficulties. Think about your own talents and struggles. How easy is it for you to change your own ideas and habits? Your child needs extra stimulus, encouragement, and repetition to foster strong development. Invite in friends and family to widen the scope of enrichment for your child. Encourage positive relationships with trusted others for your child to explore familiar and challenging tasks. The care and interest given by your loved ones helps boost skills, emotional development and deepens connection for your youngster. It will also augment the emotional intelligence and understanding of people in your wider circle. I have met many wonderful people who've described the inspiration and positive growth they have experienced in seeking to support family and friends with SEND. Having relationships full of fun and trust is what we all want

Try taking control of your thinking about possibilities for your child. Before bed or on waking up, set a scene for your day ahead in your mind and heart. Look forward to it. Imagine how the day will proceed in a positive sense, so that you already have a mental script which is very supportive of you both. This optimistic thinking and feeling about the day ahead informs your actions and helps your body. This in turn will increase your chances of success. You can understand and resonate with this child better than anyone else. You are the scene setter for your child, and you yourself will be transformed and increasingly able to appreciate the world through your child's eyes. Keep your role in mind as you create a safe, fun, and exploratory new world with your child. If aspects of your day go pear shaped, you can always try again.

Remember, you are already a superhero. You have brought this child into the world and supported them ever since they arrived in your life. You and this child are on a quest. The answers are not easy, and you will have to search hard and try against many odds to find solutions. You are already an expert in this. Trust that you will find and create what you need when you need it. Small steps make big differences. Love, care, intelligence, and understanding are your superpowers.

Practise affirmations. Realise the power of stating your intent. Affirmations are just collections of words, sentences which you use on a regular basis to boost your own mood and emotional strength. They are also useful linguistic devices to support your child. I was reluctant at first to engage with the idea of affirmations. Then I realised that just about every utterance we make is a form of affirmation. We all have brain chatter going on whilst awake, and affirmations are a conscious choice about the words we use to communicate with ourselves and others. So I gave it a go and stuck to it.

My affirmation was "I am a calm and loving parent, and I can do this." These words became increasingly helpful to me during the tough times. Affirmations worked well for our son, too. I would say to him, "Sammy is a clever and brave boy, and Sammy can do this." We were both soothed by these positive words, which became like a suit of armour as we headed into our toilet training quest.

Start with one or two sentences you repeat on a regular basis as affirmation—like, "I've got this" and "My child poos in the toilet with ease." Teach your child to sing, "I can do a poo, I do it in the loo." It may seem ridiculous, and it might not even be true yet, but the trick is to fake it till you make it. I tried this technique in a moment of desperation and was amazed when it began to work. Our son could say "poo-ooh", and we kept going with this song until the desired outcome started.

So use these suggestions and make them your own as they occur to you in your circumstances. When I decided to make conscious decisions about my inner narrative and outward speech, things started to look up. Even if it just boosted our self-esteem, it helped us both. What you say is creative and creates a new reality in your mind, heart, and eventually your experience. What have you got to lose? If that seems too New Agey, just see it as evidence of your amazing parenting skills. (This of course is true. You are amazing—look how far you've come already!) This child chose you as a great person to help them through their path in life.

As you trust yourself more and relax (I know … but it can happen!), you can allow your own creativity to bubble up. You may begin to find that everything you need begins to flow to you and from you. Your lighter mood will inevitably impact your child and improve things for them.

Your words have power. Thoughts become things. Look around you. Everything begins with a thought, including toilets. People like Thomas Crapper, who pioneered some flushing mechanisms, were inspired by the need to improve hygiene and public health for the burgeoning masses of the day. I wonder if those early pioneers imagined a world of many flushing toilets!

The Funny Way Forward

To put it simply, find joy. You can find protection and strength in cartoon-like personas. Get a theme song for the show you star in. You need a belter—I like "I Love My Life" by Robbie Williams—which raises your spirits and drives you forward in positivity and love. A song can be your pick-me-up or a switch to a different persona which supports you as the carer in a trying situation. When you love a tune and raise your own vibes, you're ready for anything. Needing to always love, love, love can be tough when you're feeling angry, confused, helpless, or plain exhausted. Trust that you are not alone. The world is full of parents who also struggle. Most of us can get a lift from a tune we love, and our children can too.

The wonderful aforementioned Robbie Williams has a performance persona he dons on stage and sees as an alter ego, a character at one remove from his own. It proved useful for us to have alternative and comical characters we could become in challenging times. I often made up funny faux characters and assumed silly voices to make our child laugh and engage. I copied the idea from our friend Sophia who is a talented performer. Sophia had studied performance with puppets. She enjoyed using a range of different accents to communicate with and entertain Sammy. One particular character, 'Bingo' was a runaway success. I imported Bingo into our family life. This character inhabited cutlery at the dinner table to start with but can morph itself into any object. "Bingo" helps with difficult transitions like moving from room to room or going through the front door in the morning. Bingo can be the voice of toys, my talking hands, and any nearby object which may be useful in the moment. For children with autism, a third-person entity can be very helpful and supportive for all concerned, making difficult situations light and funny. It has been a game changer for us on many occasions and can keep the necessary repetition from becoming stale. You can put it on like a rain jacket to protect yourself from the weather, and change back afterwards.

A well-practised alter ego can also protect you from becoming too personally distraught in the difficult moments, like a costume you can wear when you need to, an effective self-protection for frayed emotions, removing yourself from your usual thoughts and interactions.

A toy can become a character too, and take a keen interest in your child's toilet learning. The child is supported by having an encouraging friend who can explain things as a non-threatening third personality in the room. These ideas can be implemented with whatever your current needs are. For some it can start with just getting to the bathroom independently or without trauma. This transition can be very difficult for some children. I still often have to play a game of "I'm coming to get you"—my child is very motivated by chasing games and otherwise freezes quite often if asked to move location in the house or at school. We have lots of pretend play chases. This activity counteracts Sammy's tendency to freeze. Problems with transition are very common in children with autism. Parents and carers have to figure out what works. Start wherever your current needs are and build in small steps with constant reinforcement. *Keep it simple* and layer ideas into your child's thinking.

Self-Belief and Self-Care

Fear, frustration, fatigue, and overwhelm make small-feeling loners of us all. Trust that you are not alone. Right now there is at least one other human on the planet experiencing something very similar. Learn to step back from your own negative thoughts and watch them as if they were a TV drama. When you can observe your own chatter, you are no longer a prisoner to it. You are special, worthwhile, and strong. This is why you're the perfect person for your child.

This is just a moment, and all moments pass. We all have good and bad moments.

Trust that you are now in a new life which will unfold in the right way for you. Know that you can create every moment with your thoughts, words, and actions. You can always choose your reaction to events. In addition to being an amazing parent or carer, you have to care for yourself too. Create habits and routines which nourish you. I have created a kit of ideas and activities for your child to use with you which encourage engagement and independence in the task of toilet learning. It's likely that you will need to be a very active and leading participant here. You will provide the skills your child does not yet have. Keep going and believe in progress.

Look for what raises your vibrations and makes you feel good. You have a calling card to pursue a road less travelled. Your companions on this journey are likely to have strong, kind hearts, curious minds, and imagination. You're about to learn a whole load of stuff you didn't know existed. You can and will do it and are likely meet some of the most amazing people you've ever come across.

My Ten Commandments

When caring for a child with SEND, it's easy to lose sight of your self-care. These "commandments" are meant to be succinct reminders you can copy, print out, laminate, and post in the toilet with you. You could load them onto your mobile phone—anywhere they'll be a useful reminder.

Thou shalt ...

1. **breathe.** You and your child are on a superhero journey. A deep breath in and out places you in the "now".

2. **experience space and time.** You're in charge together. There is no rush, and all is well. You've got this.

3. **remember to smile.** Try to see the humour. Keep actions and language light. No pressure.

4. **invite, encourage, support, and empower.** Use your body awareness, mediation training, affirmations, and songs.

5. **reinforce** your child's learning with gentleness. You have a reassuring but flexible routine which you can adjust as you go along.

6. **breeze over difficulties.** Minimise bad feelings.

7. **use your tools.** Songs, toys, memory games, and affirmations create positive, fun learning.

8. **praise your child's effort**, even if it seems messy or is just a halting step forward.

9. **praise yourself.** You're still here and trying.

10. **chart and reward significant milestones.** Use certificates or other awards to reinforce a sense of achievement and your child's desire for improvement.

To the Child

Read this section aloud to your child. Think about your answers together. There is a lot here so choose the parts which work for you.

Dear learner,

You are amazing. Your *parents and carers* love you and know you are fantastic. Show them your wonderful learning skills and how brave you are in trying new things.

1. What are some new things you've tried recently? Your parent or carer will help you write, draw or stick a picture of it here.

You are a superhero because you've made it here. You have met and beaten many challenges. You are living proof that you can beat the odds. Well done so far!

Checklist of how good I am already

How good am I and where am I going? Let's check off some of the hard things you've learned to do:

- ➔ learned to communicate
- ➔ show love
- ➔ be funny
- ➔ play
- ➔ walk
- ➔ talk
- ➔ run
- ➔ make friends
- ➔ go to school

What hard things have you learned to do ?

AMANDA SMIGIELSKI

Here's a space where we can draw or paste in a picture of you being a superhero and doing something hard. Your parent or carer will help you select a picture.

Wow! Well done.

THE BOOK OF POO

To the Child
Pit Stop Checklist Ideas

Now we have one more challenge you can meet. You're going to become a toilet champion! Draw a picture or stick a sticker about being a PIT toilet champion. Ask your carer to help you.

My Survival Kit

You can do it! This is your very own survival kit that you can pack with tools you need.(Carer, you know the level of support which is appropriate here. Provide the level of support needed. Your child can use the skills of speech, literacy and drawing which they have to respond to and show understanding of the ideas here. Some challenge is always helpful for learning. On the other hand, you will be sensitive to how daunted your child may feel with some challenges. You will be able to adjust tasks accordingly.)

My Team

You have your own superhero team at home to help you. They are going to be with you and get there with you.

Do you know who's on your team? Let's find out.

1. Who is on your team at home? Do you have a parent or carers? Do you have brothers or sisters? That's your superhero team. How do they help you?

2. Who is on your team at school? Do you have teachers and TAs? Do you have a school support therapists? What about friends? That's your school team.

3. Do you have other helpers or carers outside school? What about therapists? That's your support team?

4. Do you have doctors and nurses who help you to take care of your body? Do you have a physical therapist? That's your medical support team.

5. Most of all, you have yourself, the superstar hero!

AMANDA SMIGIELSKI

6. Everyone on your team believes you can do it!

My Music

You can use a song or a rhyme to support your body. Here's a song:

> I can do it, I can poo.
> I can do it, I can poo.
> I can do it, I can poo.
> I can do it in the loo.
> Who can poo in the loo?
> Me, me, me and you can too.

If you like this song, you can share it with your parents and carers. You can play instruments with it, like shakers and drums. Can you make up your own song or poem?

AMANDA SMIGIELSKI

My Art and Toys

You can choose your pictures; PECS style cards, word cards, and toys to help you. Do you have a favourite toilet toy? You can make that toy your Captain Communicator.

This is your toilet, and you're going to boss it!

Now you have your own songs, sounds, chants, and objects to help you and support the brilliant job you're doing.

If you like to draw, you can draw and paste some pictures here in the way you like. Then you have your own kit to help you.

My Affirmations

Note to parents and carers: *Even if your child is non-verbal, they can begin to think these ideas. Practise the word "ease" with them. Associate it with comfort, relaxation, and success.*

Affirmations are words I say out loud to teach my brain and body. I am learning, and I am amazing. I can achieve anything I want to.

I get to the toilet with ease.

I sit on the toilet with ease.

I wee on the toilet with ease.

I poo on the toilet with ease.

Memory Training

My mind and my muscles know how to remember.

When I go sit on the toilet, I think about _____ .

When I sit on the toilet, I ask my body to _____ .

My wee goes from my body into the _____ .

My poo goes from body into the _____ .

Here are some other things to remember about poo in the loo:

AMANDA SMIGIELSKI

BOX for doodle or writing

Visual Resources

The graphics on the pages below are ones which I designed and used to support toilet learning for Sammy. These were helpful for him to express what he was experiencing and to support the growth of his understanding. Learning and communicating information about emotions and physical sensations can be supported with these visual supports.

AMANDA SMIGIELSKI

HELP ME

CONFUSED

TUMMY ACHE

ANGRY

THE BOOK OF POO

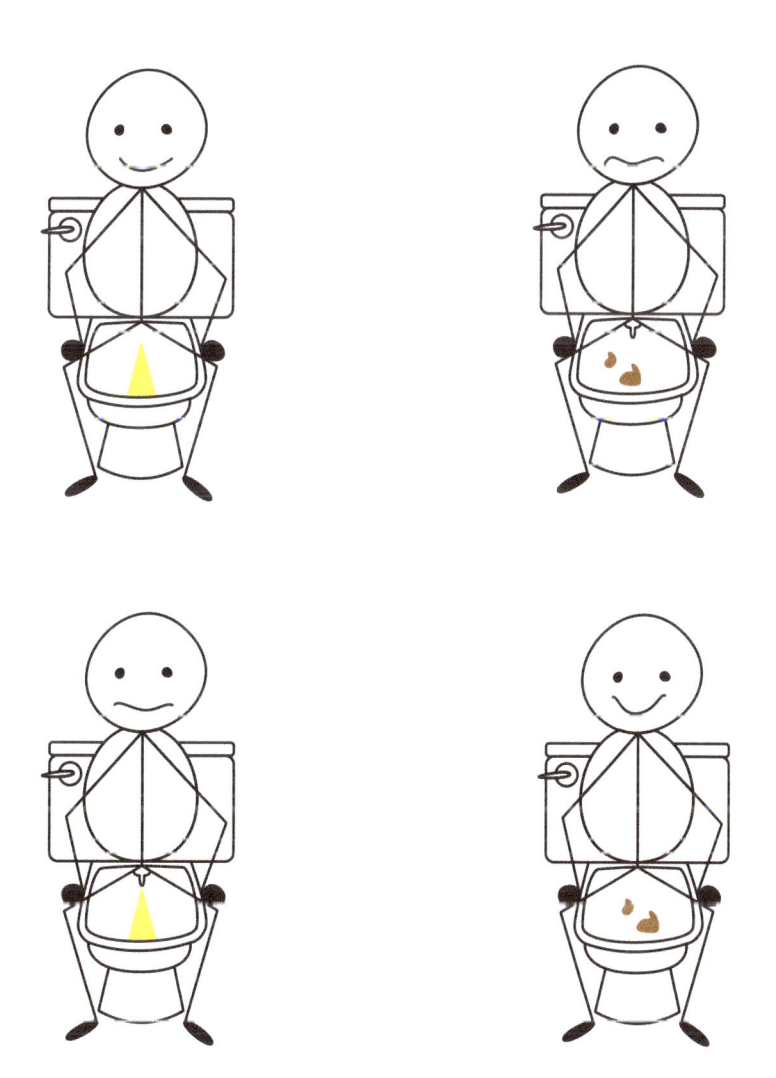

AFTERWORD

Now you have a collection of ideas and observations. You can move forwards with toilet learning with your child. You have thought deeply about barriers to learning for your child and how you can help to overcome them. You have more knowledge about what works best for both of you. You've made a real achievement in your lives. With your skills and some good luck, you can look forward to the joys which lie ahead.

As I write, I have given minimal toileting support to my 13-year-old child this week. He has been able to achieve some of his own personal care to a good level, including showering. This is a good week so far. Some weeks, for Sammy; much more care, support, and cleaning help is needed. Sammy's wonderful dad is the main go-to person for an end-of-day check and clean-up, so that appropriate social sensibility is instilled.

Even two years ago, our current situation seemed like a pipe dream, but now we're living (mostly) the dream. I hope you can use ideas here to support your own quest to improve the independence of your child, and I wish you love and light in in your thoughts, feelings, and experience.

Now, the next move for us is successful tooth brushing!

Milton Keynes UK
Ingram Content Group UK Ltd.
UKHW052131151024
449634UK00005B/19